Samuelism

C Starts With Cookie

CINDY GOH

CONTENTS:

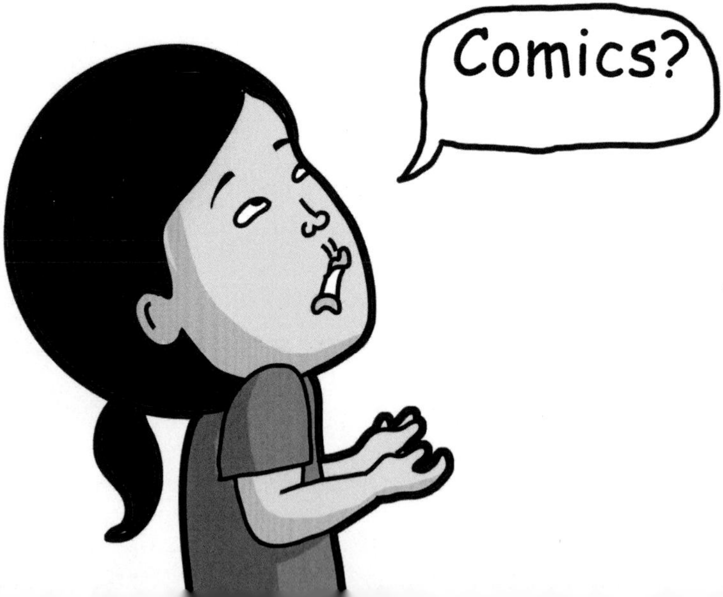
Comics?

To my kids - Nathan, Samuel, Jordyn and Rylee.
Without whom this book would have no content but I would
probably have a lot more money.

And to my husband, Raymond, for supporting me so I don't have
to get a real job.

May all of your wildest dreams come true.

CAST OF CHARACTERS

Samuel
Jordyn
Mom
Nathan
Rylee
Dad
Ponyo

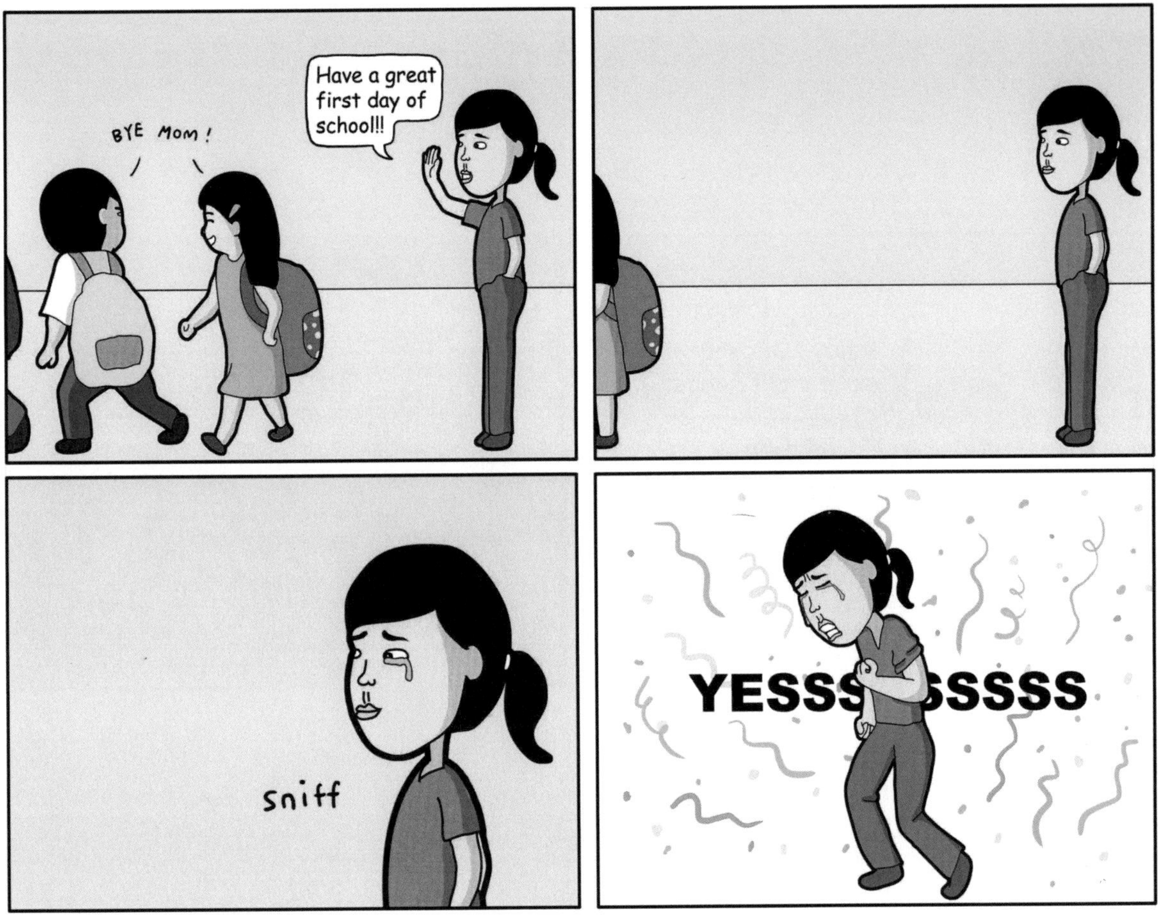
BYE MOM!
Have a great first day of school!!!
sniff
YESSSSSSSSS

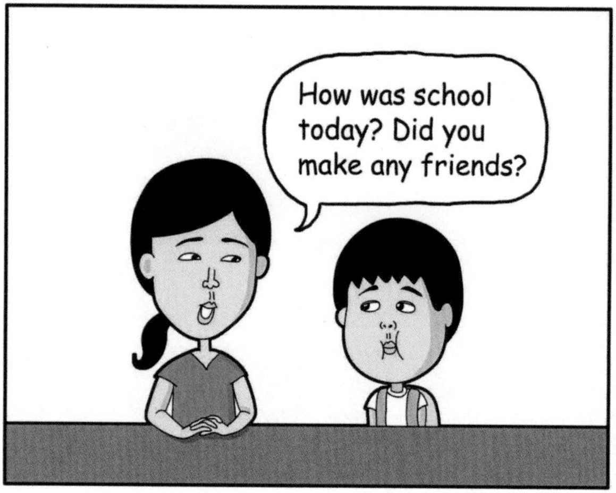
How was school today? Did you make any friends?

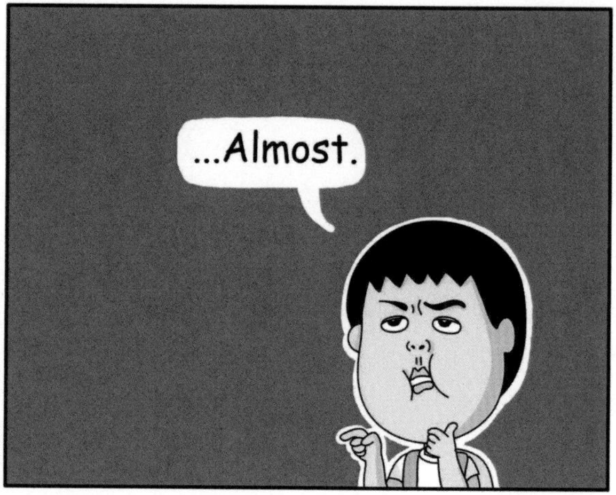
...Almost.

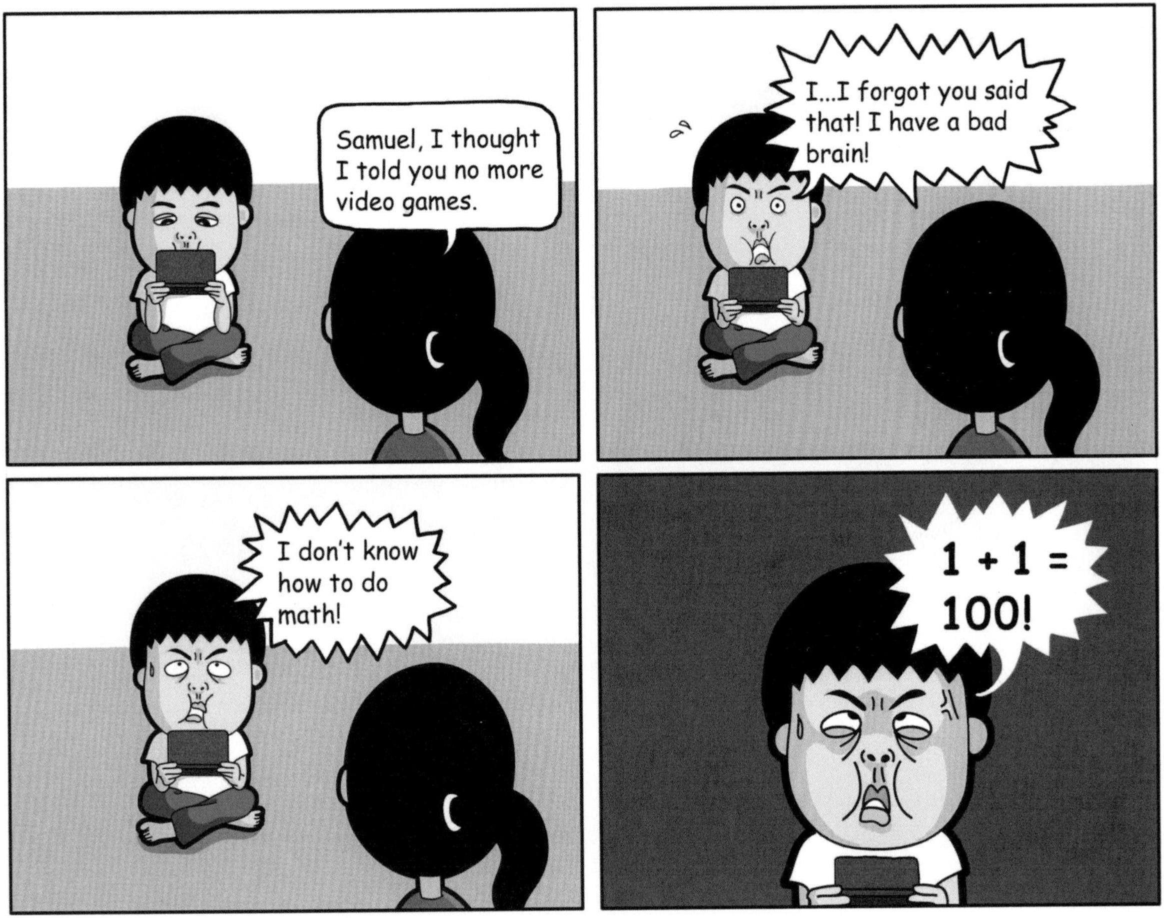
Samuel, I thought I told you no more video games.
I...I forgot you said that! I have a bad brain!
I don't know how to do math!
1 + 1 = 100!

Samuel, time to write your journal.
30 minutes later
Are you done writing? Let me see it.
Today is Thursday, tomorrow will be Friday.

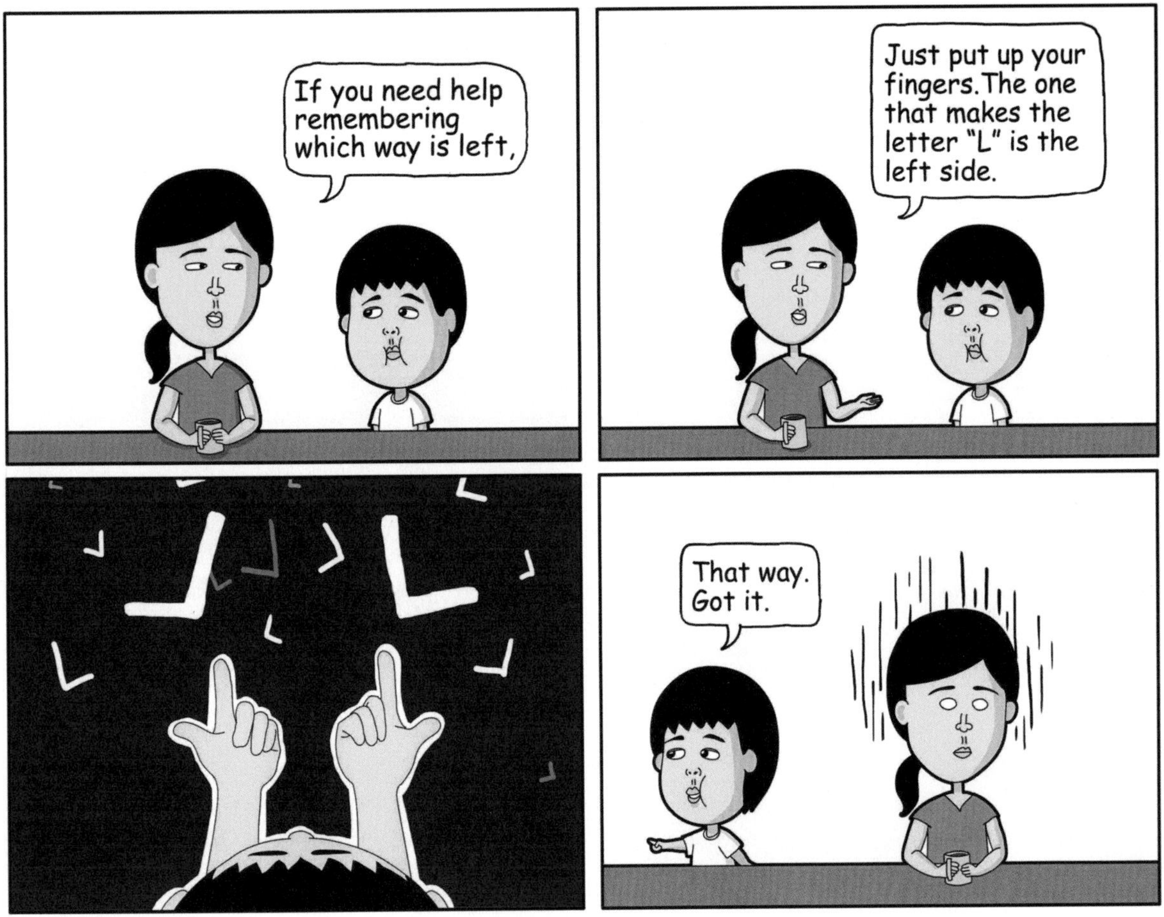
If you need help remembering which way is left,
Just put up your fingers. The one that makes the letter "L" is the left side.
That way. Got it.

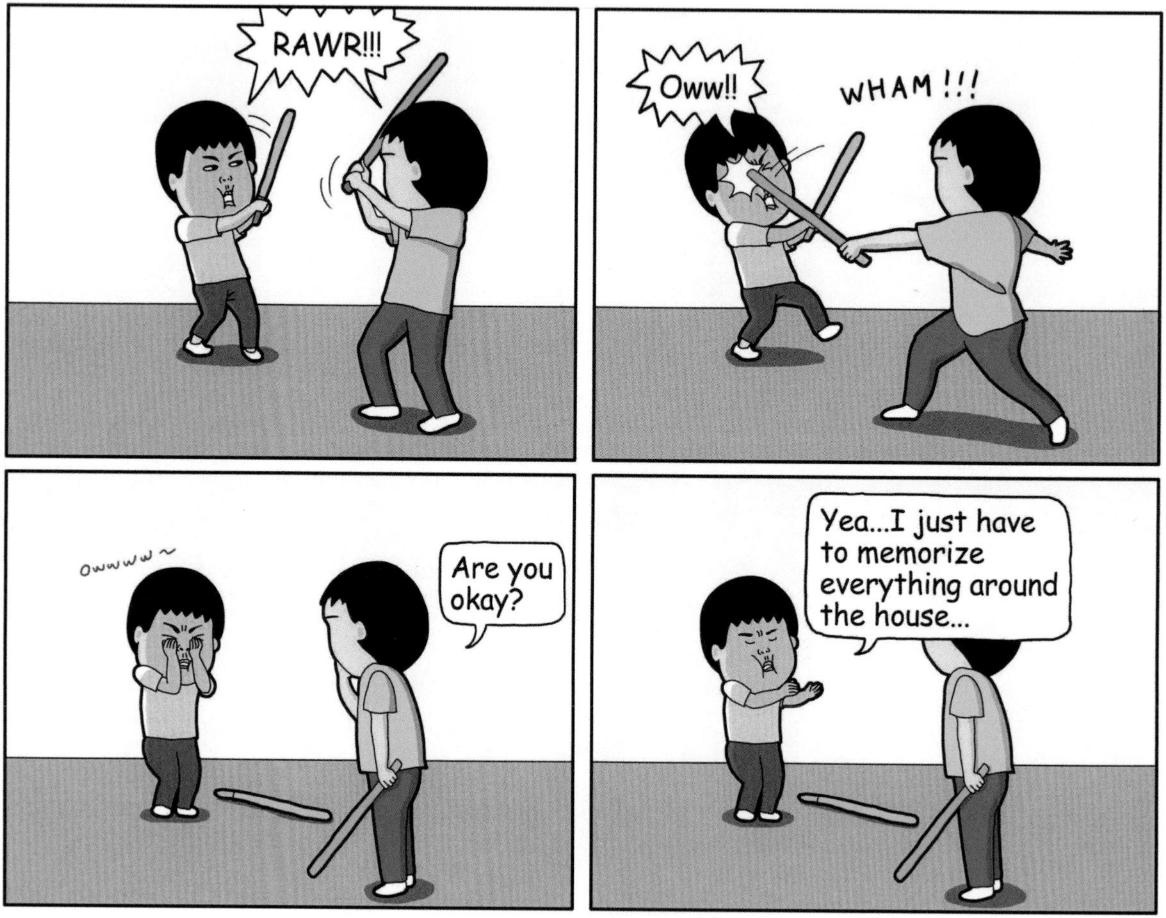
RAWR!!!
Oww!!
WHAM!!!
owwww~
Are you okay?
Yea...I just have to memorize everything around the house...

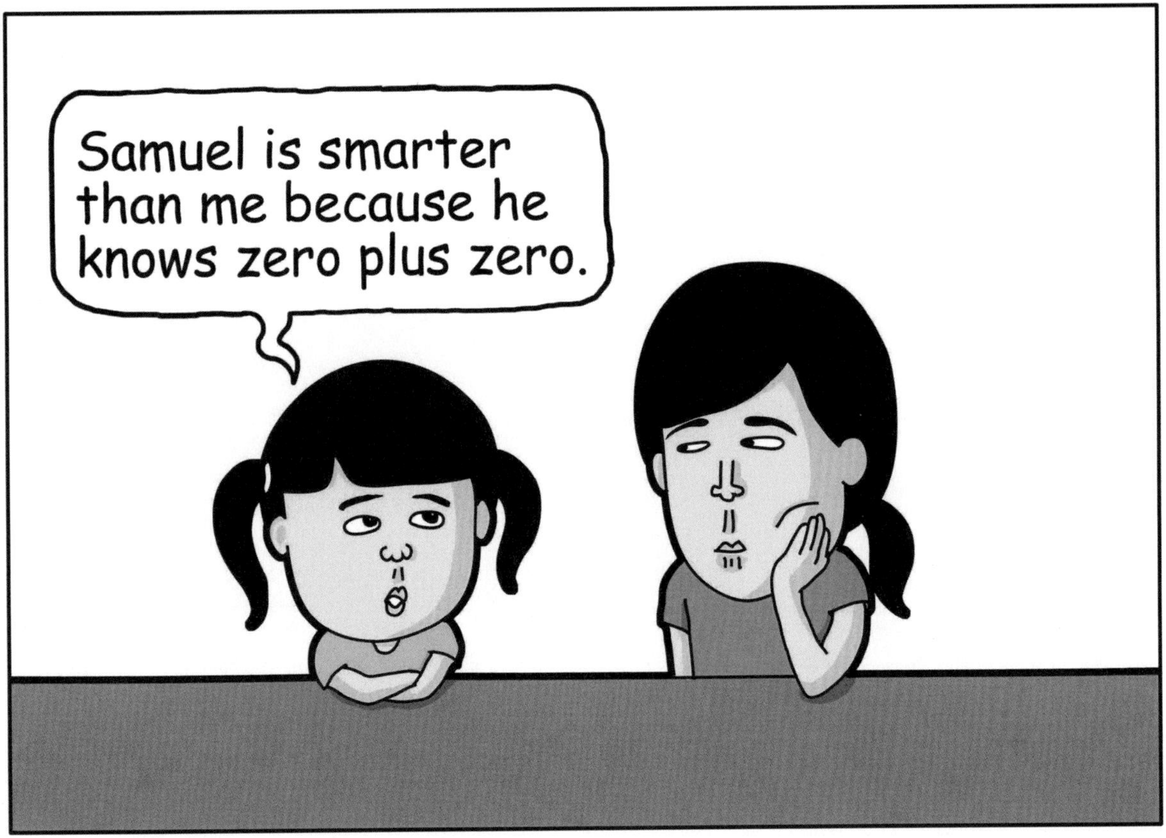
Samuel is smarter than me because he knows zero plus zero.

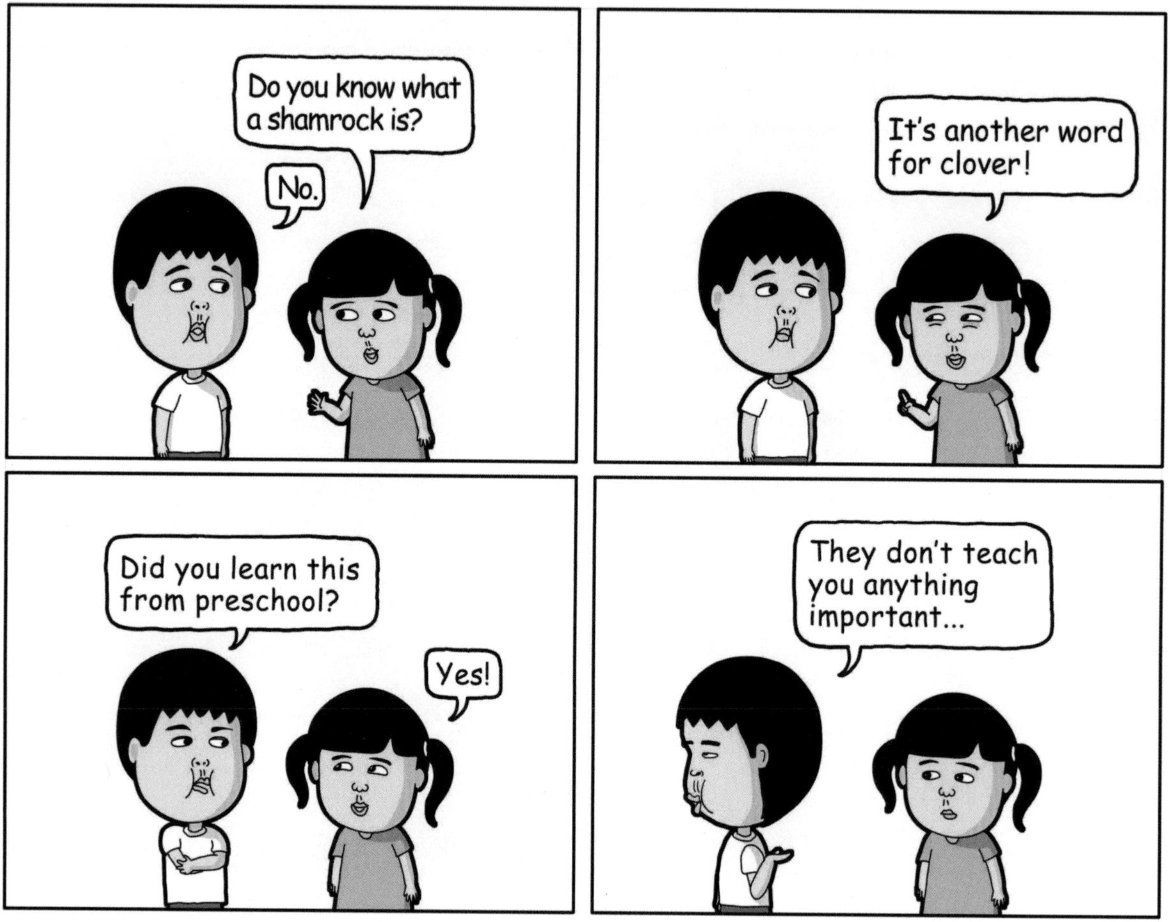
Do you know what a shamrock is?
No.
It's another word for clover!
Did you learn this from preschool?
Yes!
They don't teach you anything important...

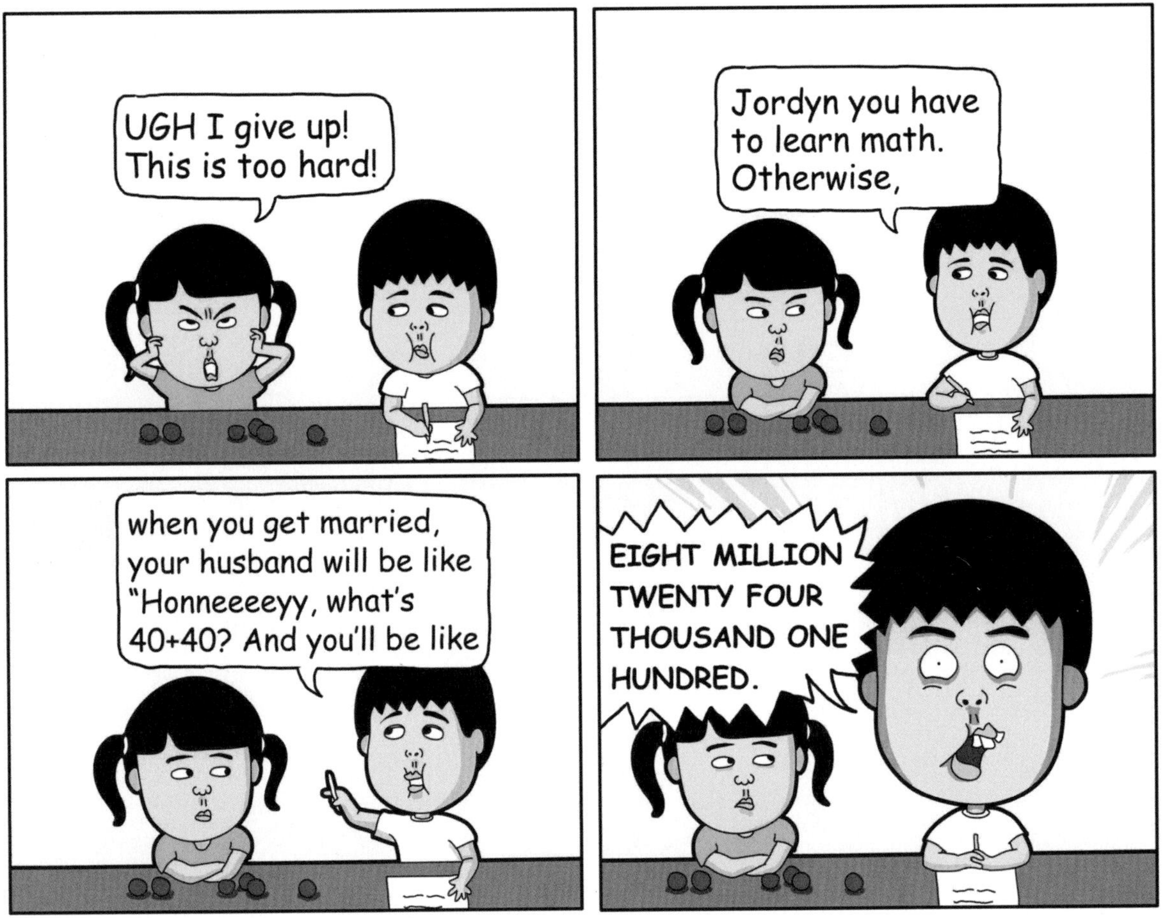
UGH I give up! This is too hard!
Jordyn you have to learn math. Otherwise,
when you get married, your husband will be like "Honneeeeyy, what's 40+40? And you'll be like
EIGHT MILLION TWENTY FOUR THOUSAND ONE HUNDRED.

Ouch
Ouch
...
Ouch

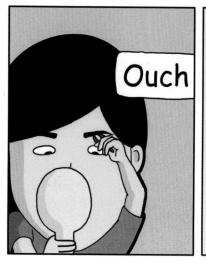

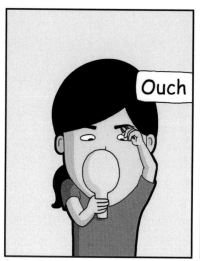

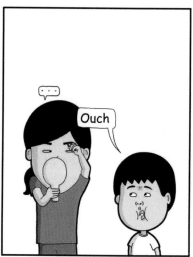

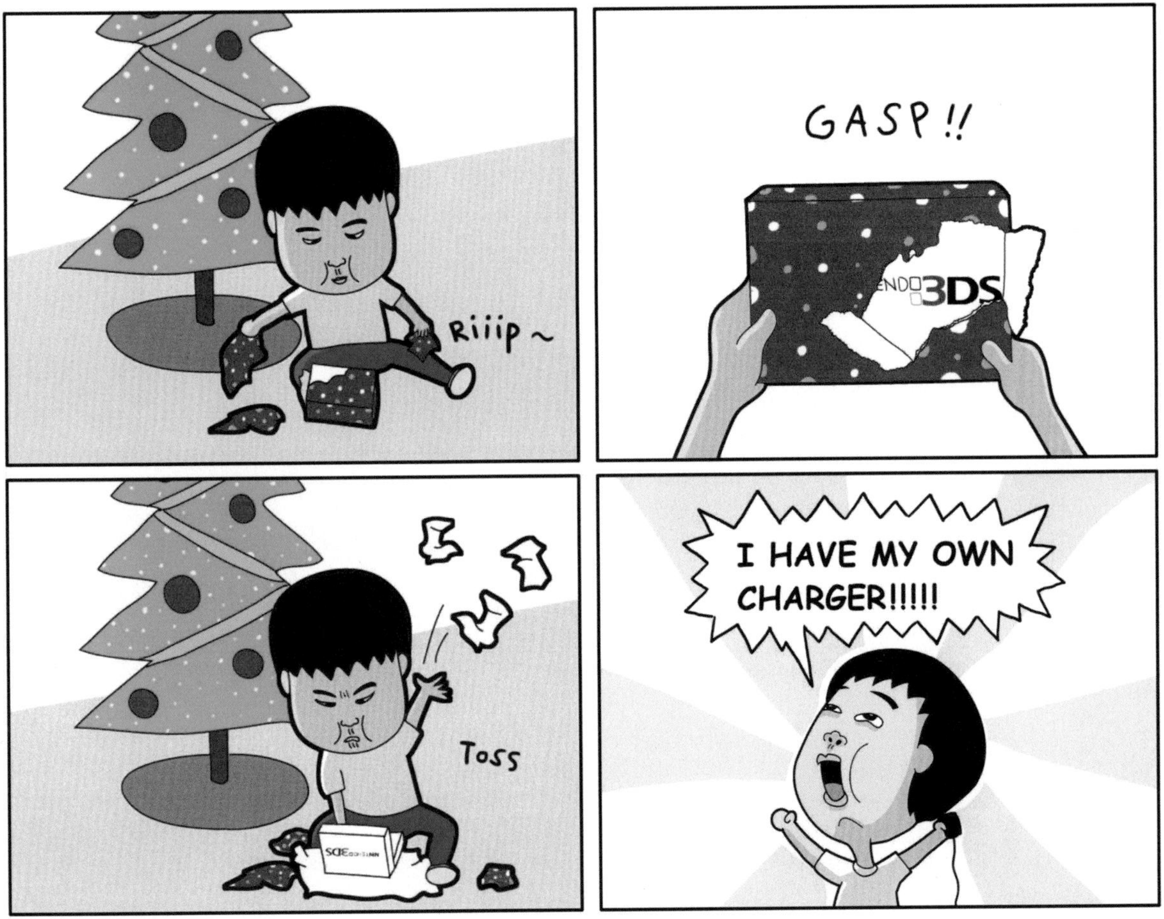
Riiip ~
GASP !!
3DS
Toss
I HAVE MY OWN CHARGER!!!!!

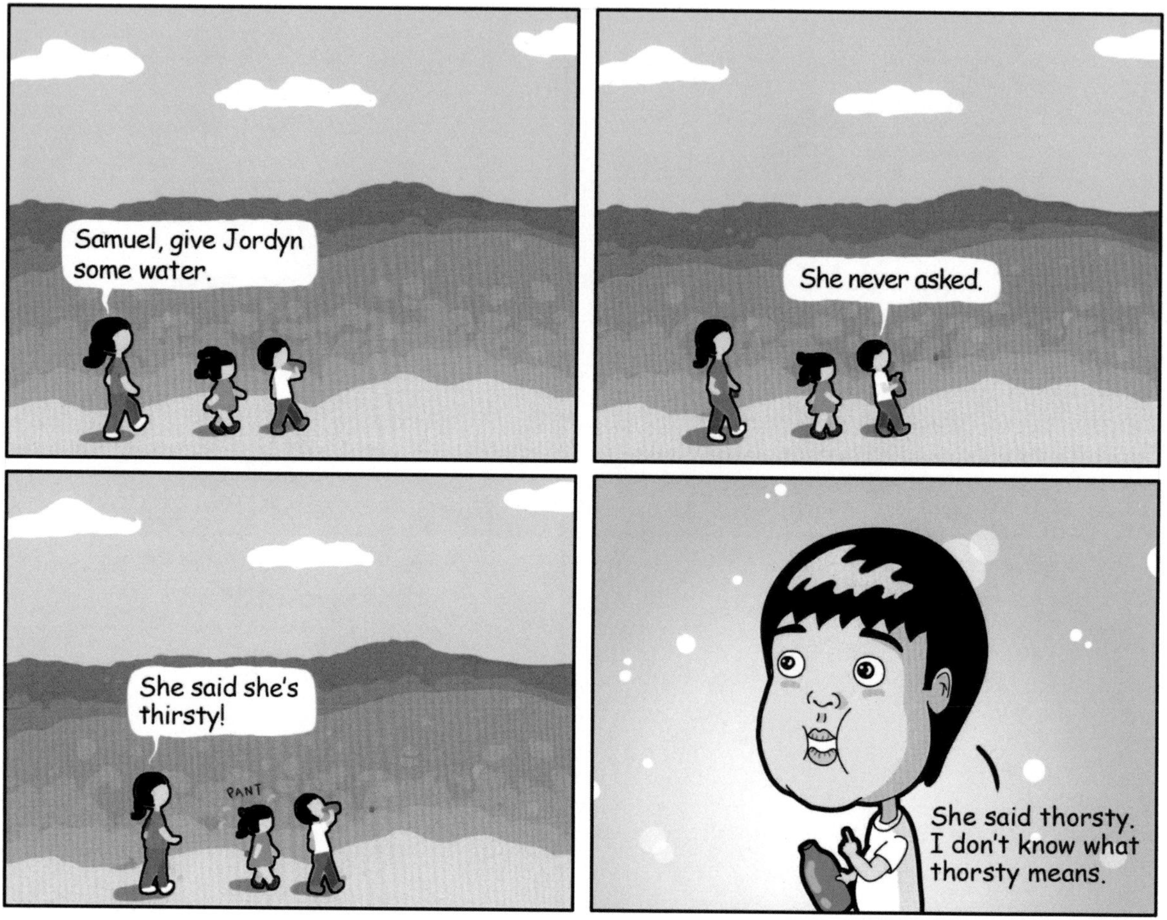
Samuel, give Jordyn some water.
She never asked.
She said she's thirsty!
PANT
She said thorsty. I don't know what thorsty means.

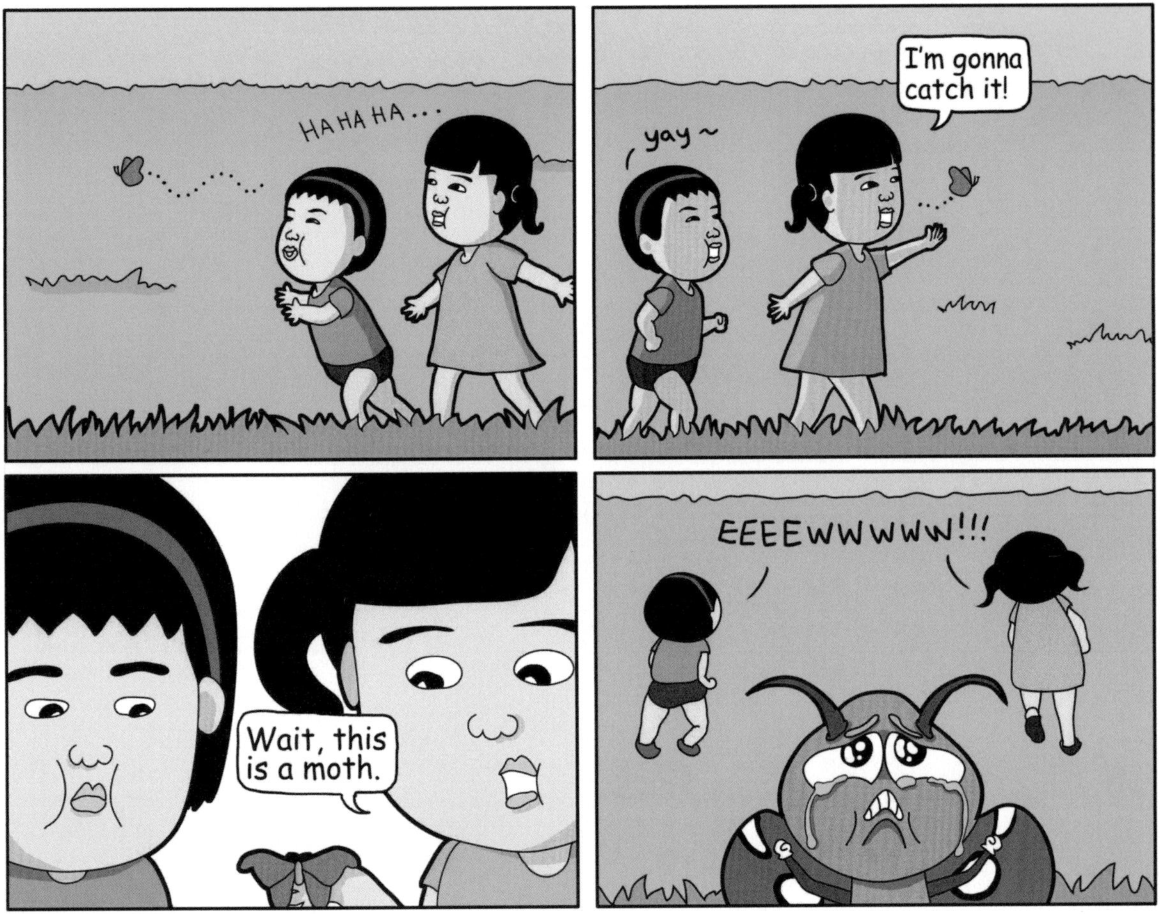
HAHAHA...
yay ~
I'm gonna catch it!
Wait, this is a moth.
EEEEWWWWW!!!

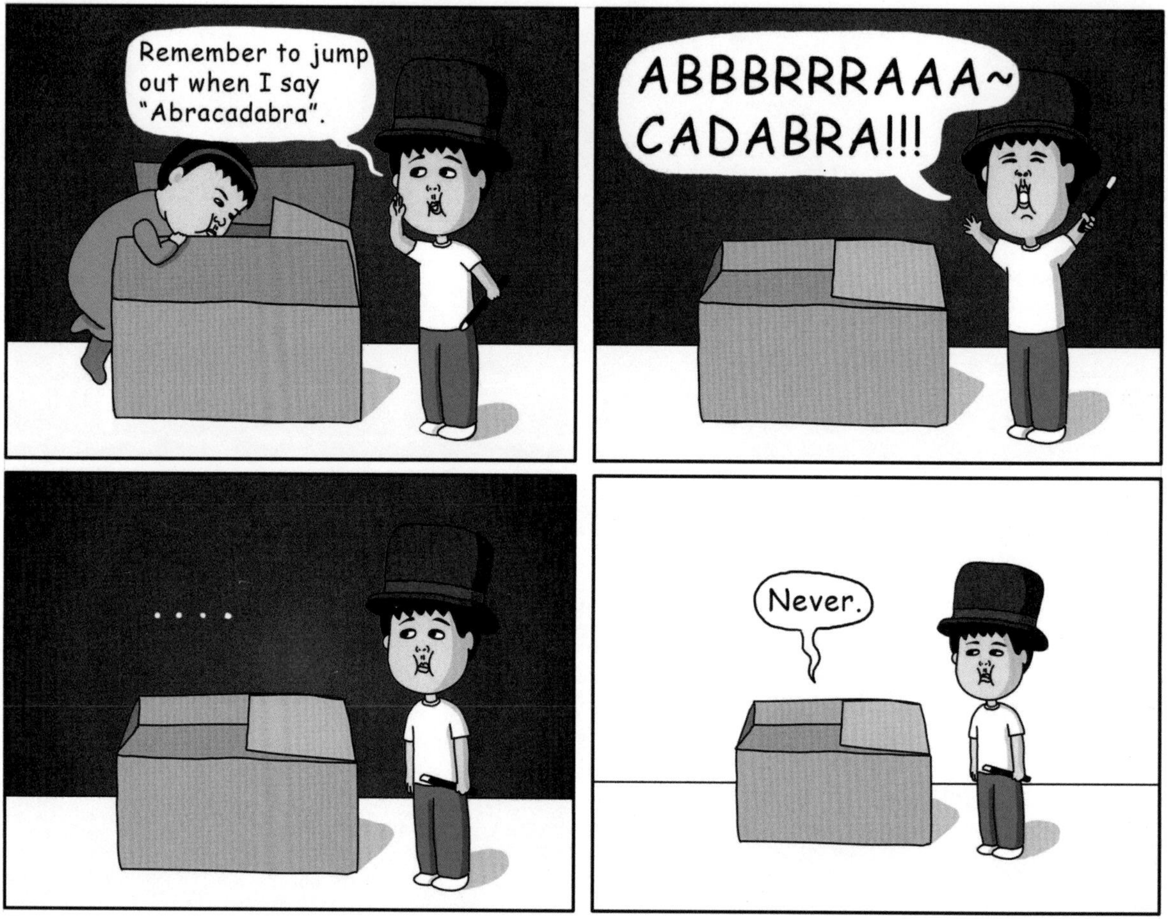
Remember to jump out when I say "Abracadabra".
ABBBRRRAAA~ CADABRA!!!
. . . .
Never.

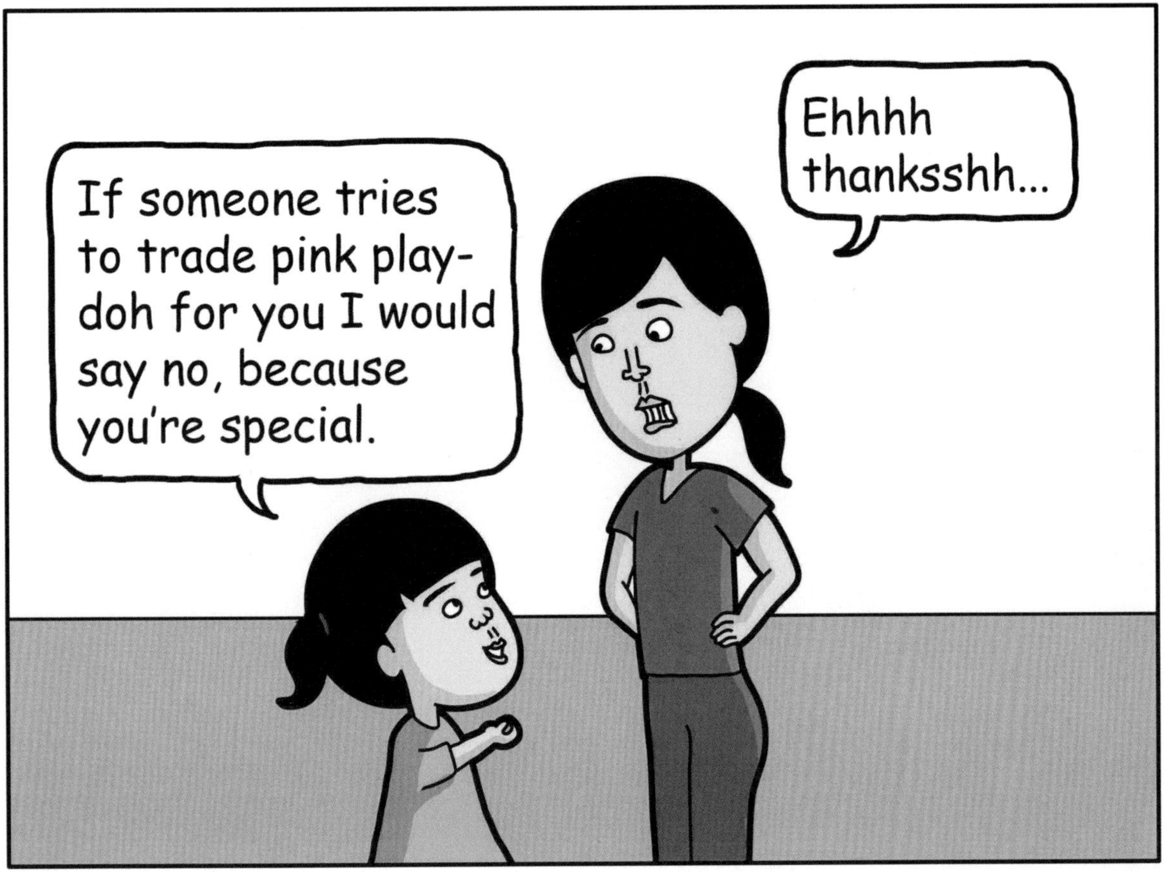
If someone tries to trade pink play-doh for you I would say no, because you're special.
Ehhhh thanksshh...

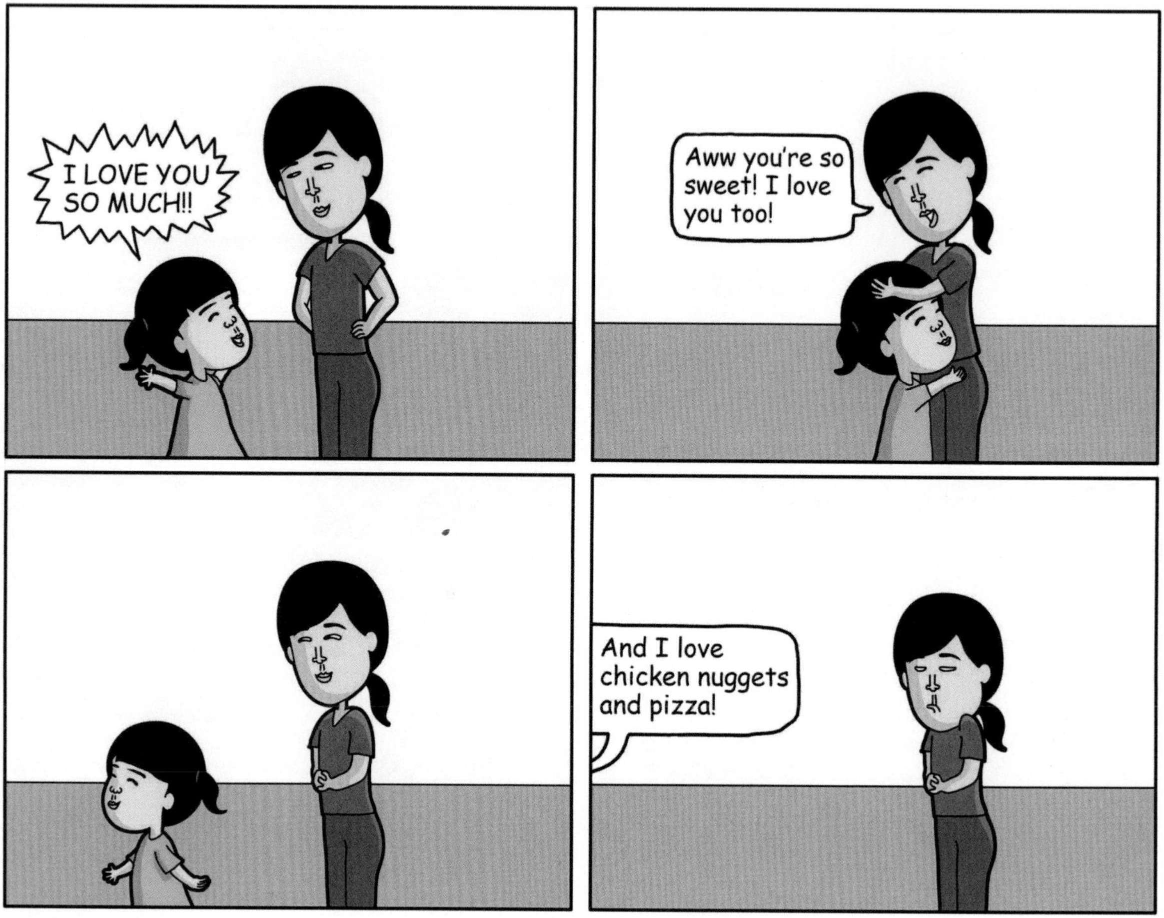
I LOVE YOU SO MUCH!!
Aww you're so sweet! I love you too!
And I love chicken nuggets and pizza!

OUCH!!
SMACK
Shhhh...

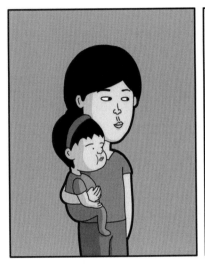

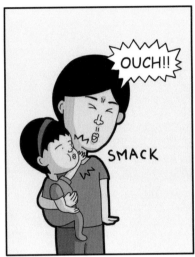

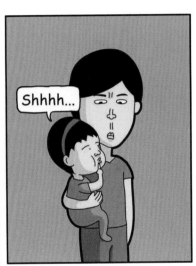

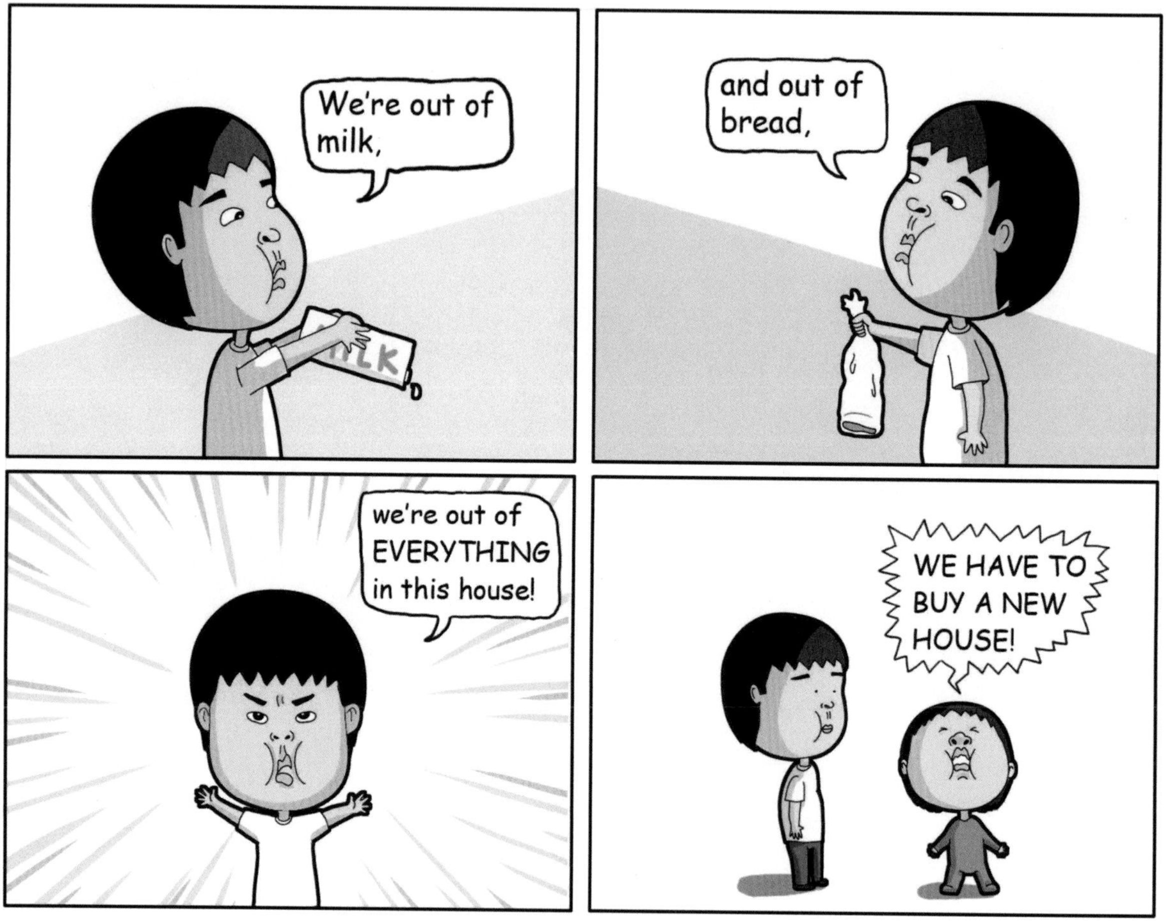
We're out of milk,
MILK
and out of bread,
we're out of EVERYTHING in this house!
WE HAVE TO BUY A NEW HOUSE!

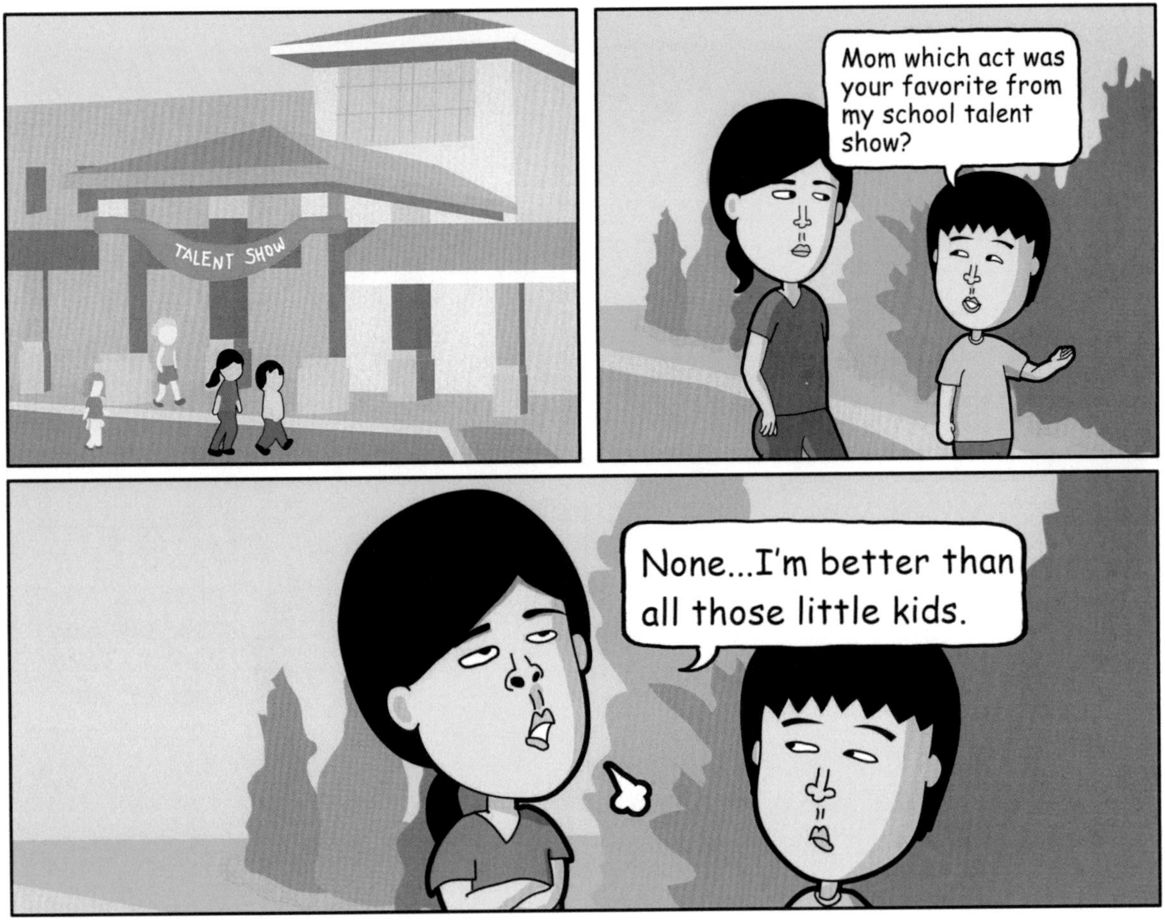
TALENT SHOW
Mom which act was your favorite from my school talent show?
None...I'm better than all those little kids.

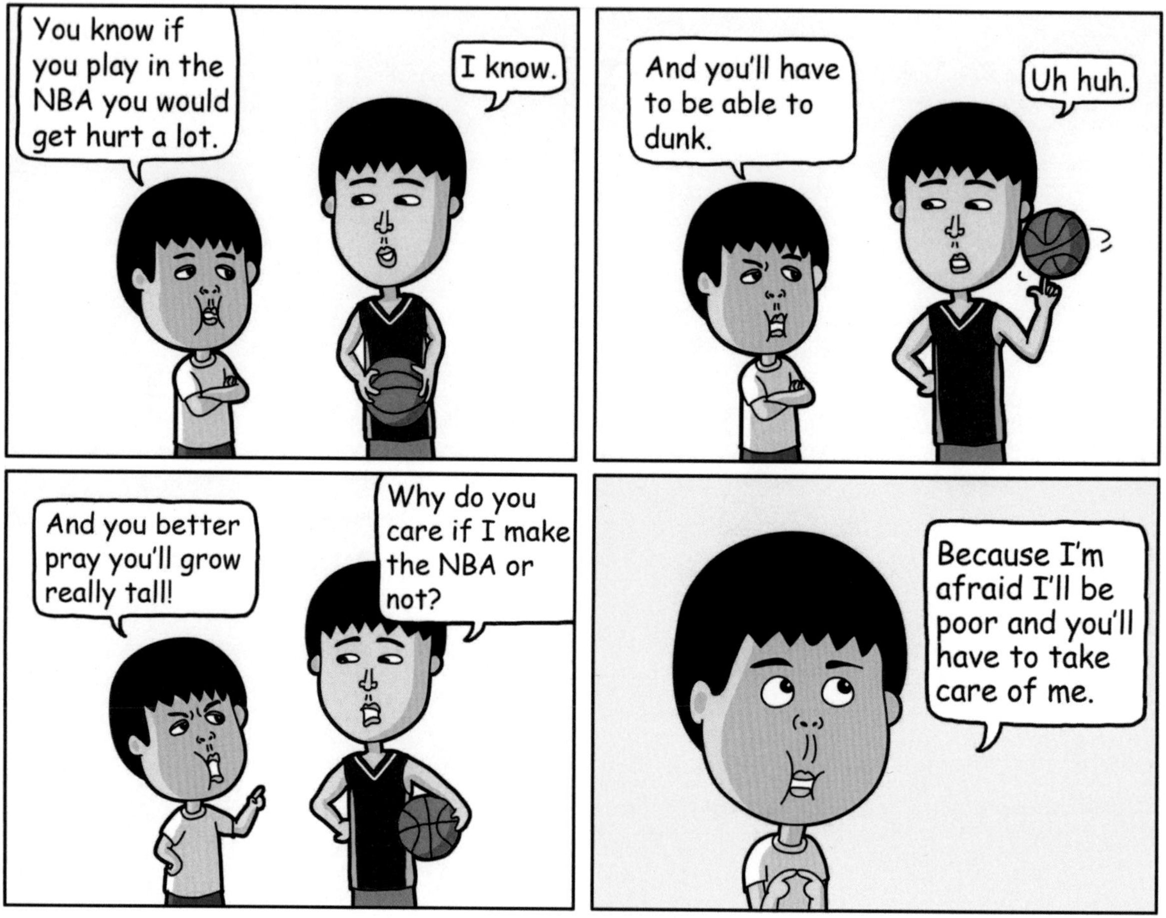

You know if you play in the NBA you would get hurt a lot.
I know.
And you'll have to be able to dunk.
Uh huh.
And you better pray you'll grow really tall!
Why do you care if I make the NBA or not?
Because I'm afraid I'll be poor and you'll have to take care of me.

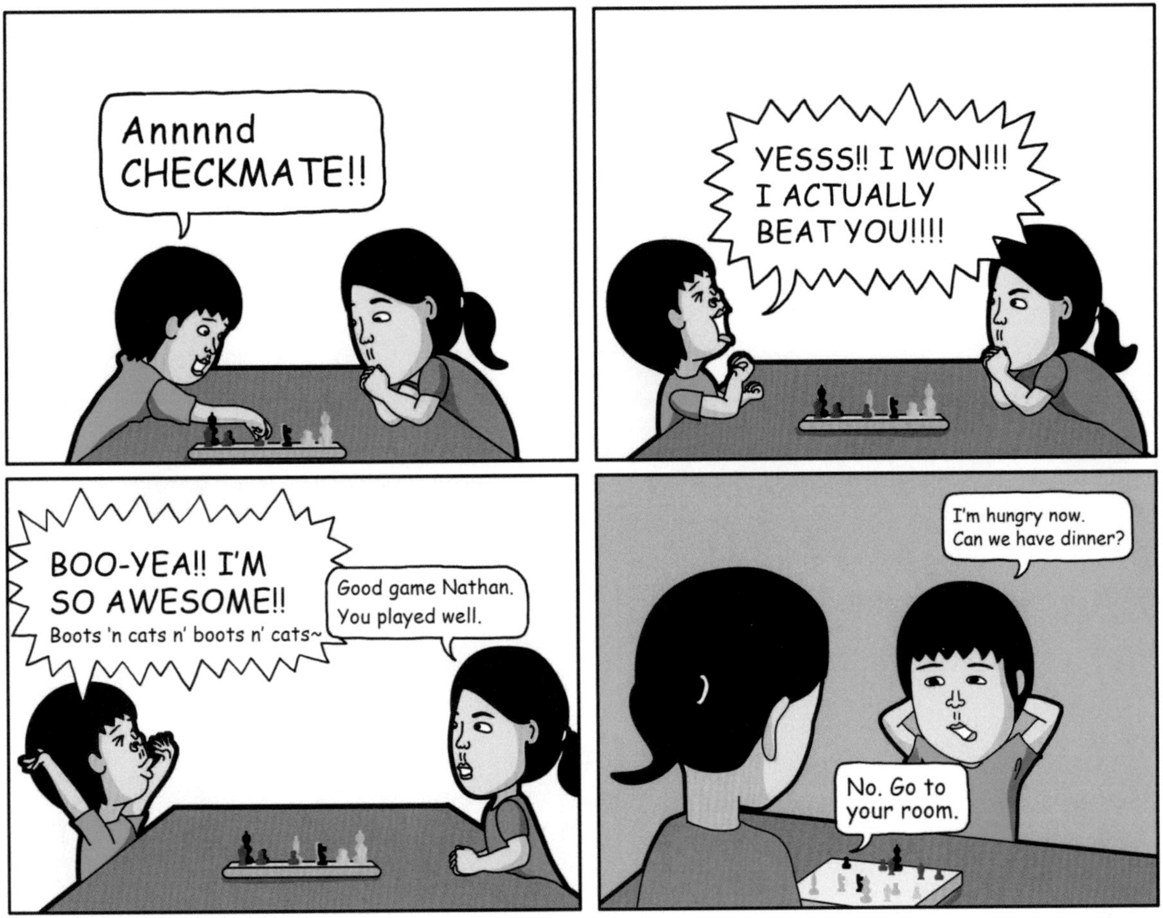
Annnnd CHECKMATE!!
YESSS!! I WON!!! I ACTUALLY BEAT YOU!!!!
BOO-YEA!! I'M SO AWESOME!!
Boots 'n cats n' boots n' cats~
Good game Nathan. You played well.
I'm hungry now. Can we have dinner?
No. Go to your room.

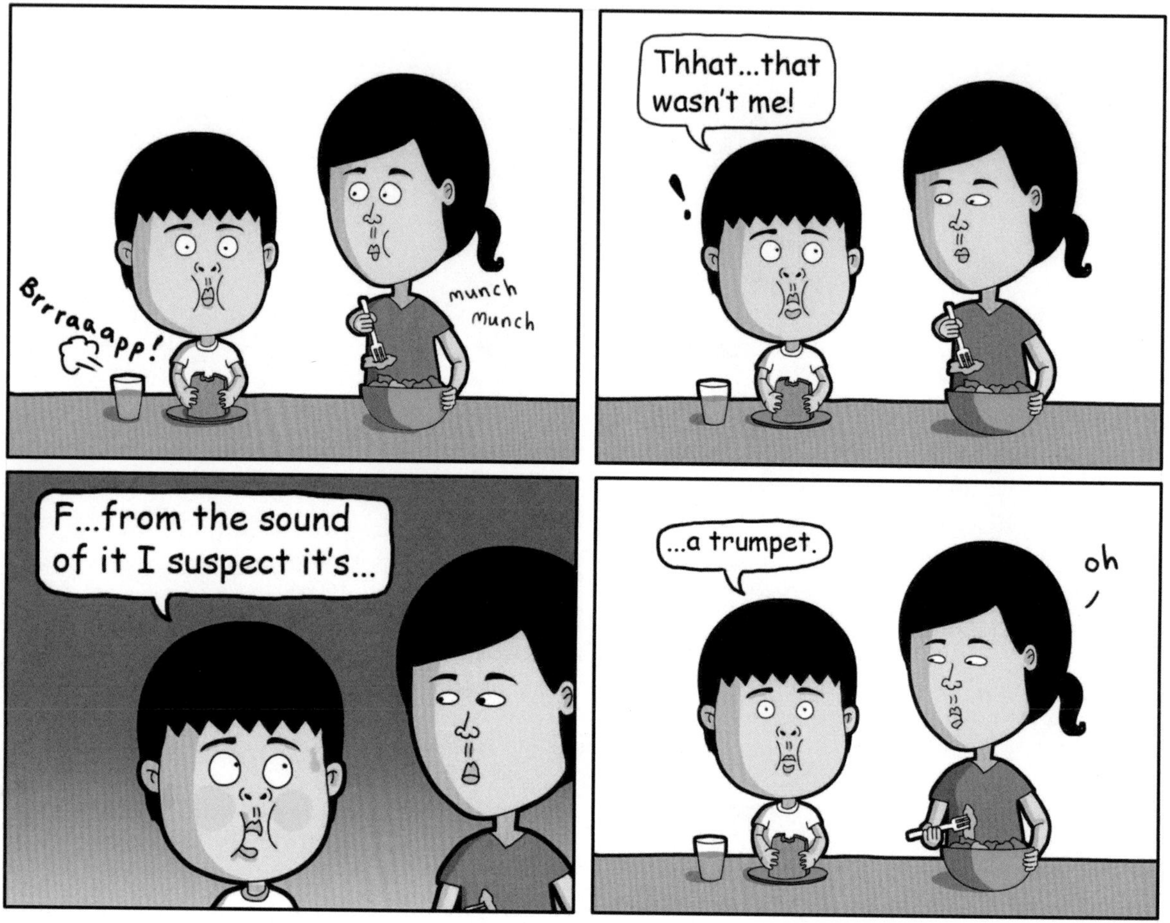
Brrraaaapp!
munch
munch
Thhat...that wasn't me!
!
F...from the sound of it I suspect it's...
...a trumpet.
oh

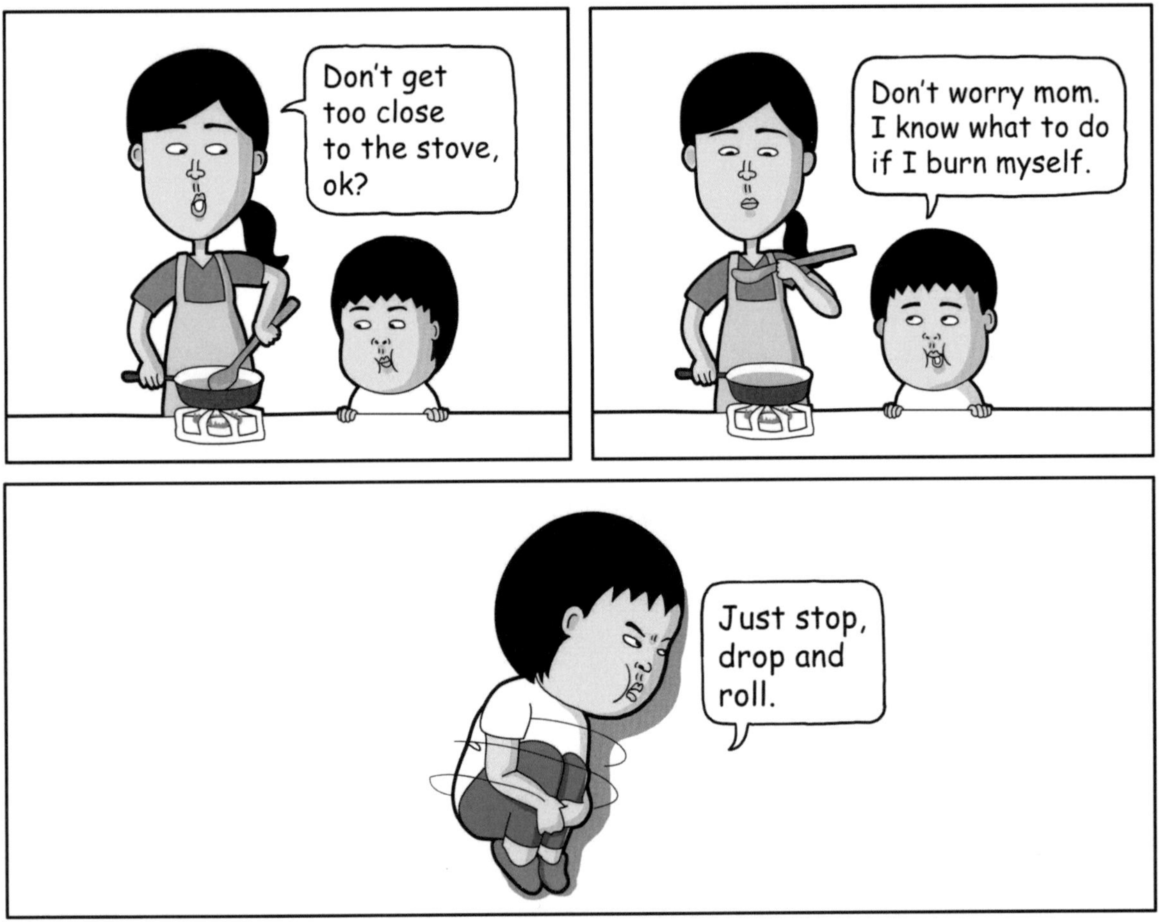
Don't get too close to the stove, ok?
Don't worry mom. I know what to do if I burn myself.
Just stop, drop and roll.

Mommy I finished all my school work on time today and I didn't even have to use the egg timer!
That's great! I knew you could do it!
Yea. What's the egg timer for anyway? It must be for good luck.

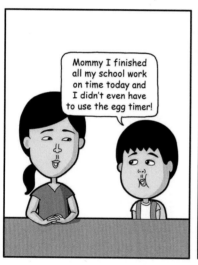

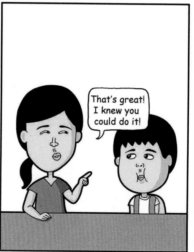

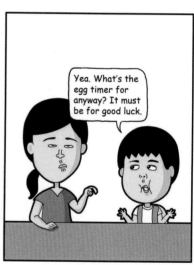

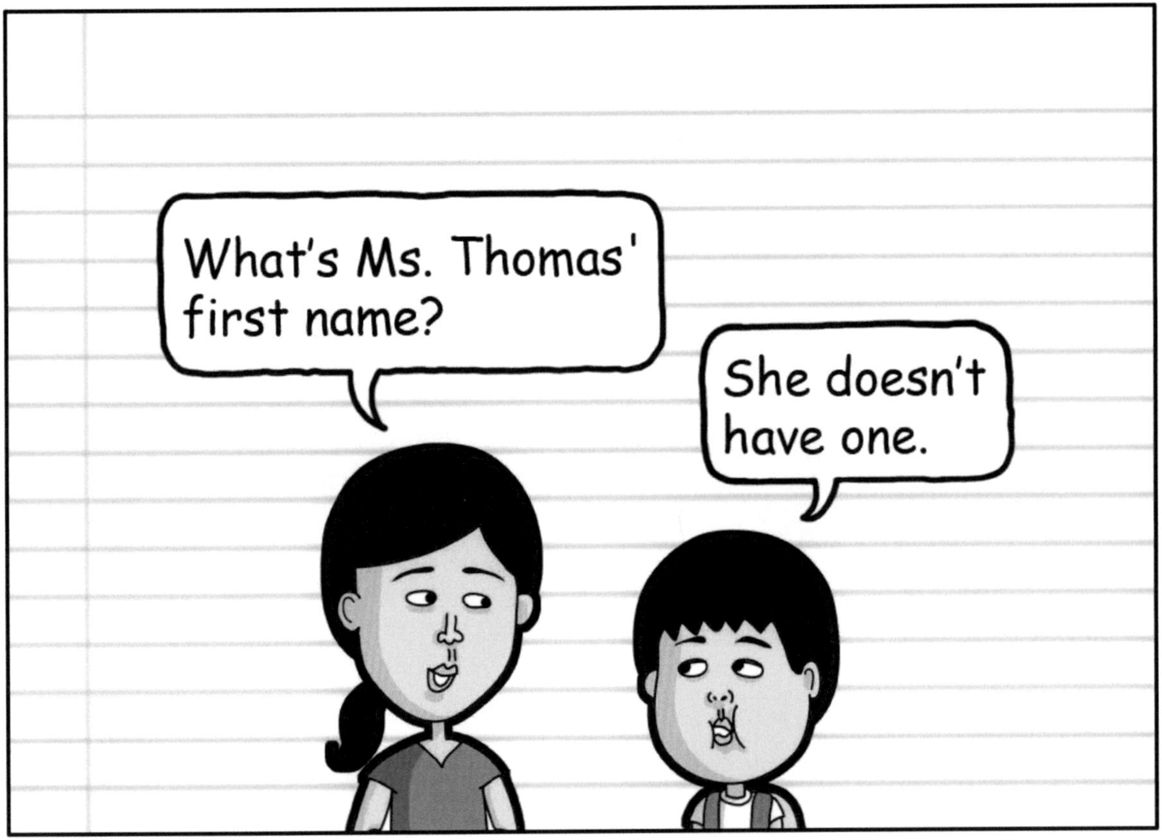
What's Ms. Thomas' first name?
She doesn't have one.

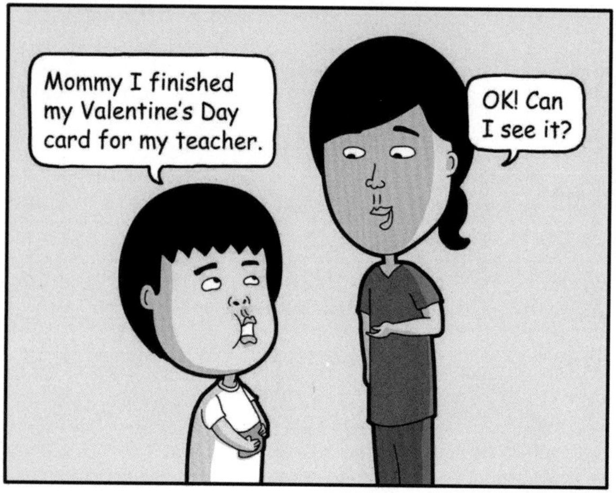
Mommy I finished my Valentine's Day card for my teacher.
OK! Can I see it?

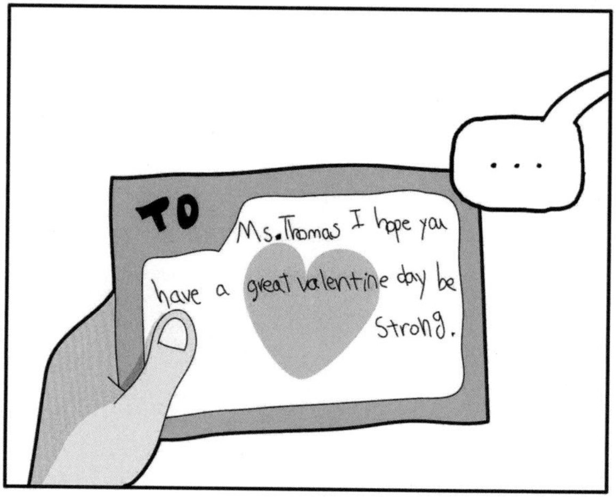
...
TO
Ms.Thomas I hope you have a great valentine day be Strong.

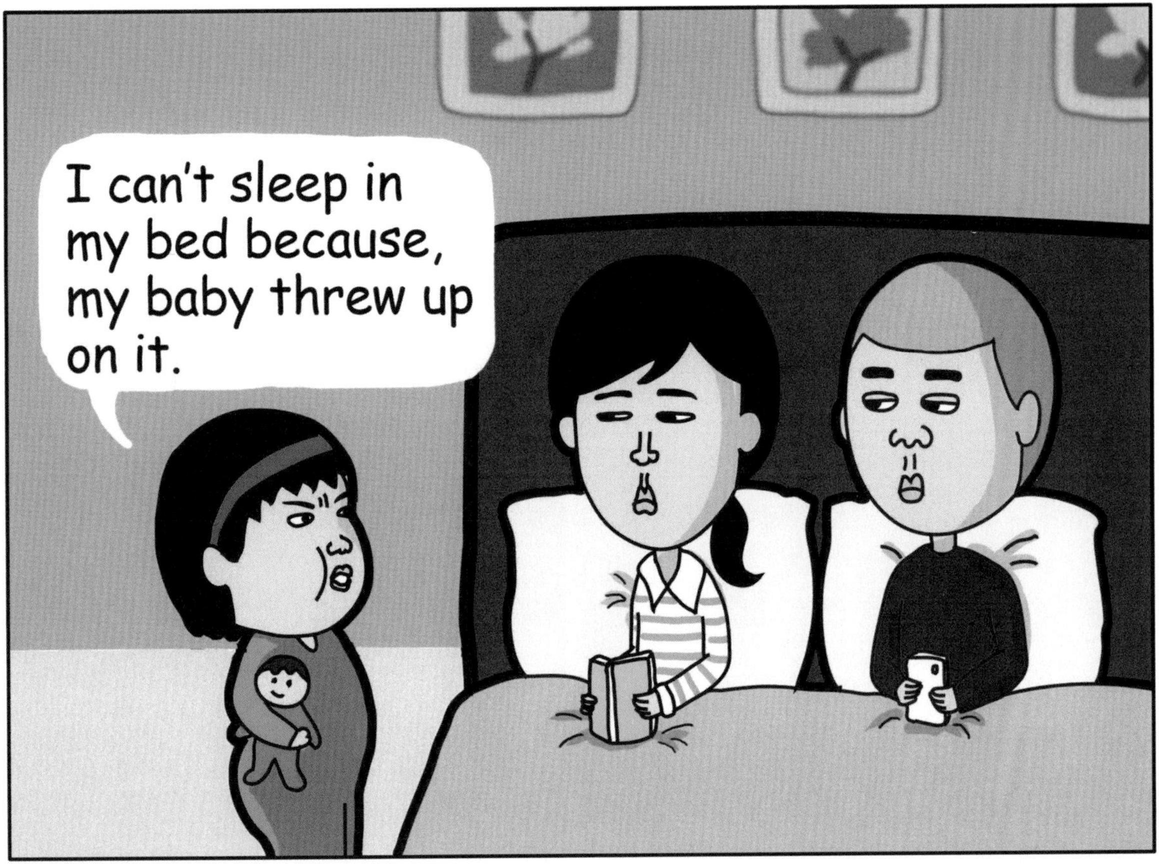
I can't sleep in my bed because, my baby threw up on it.

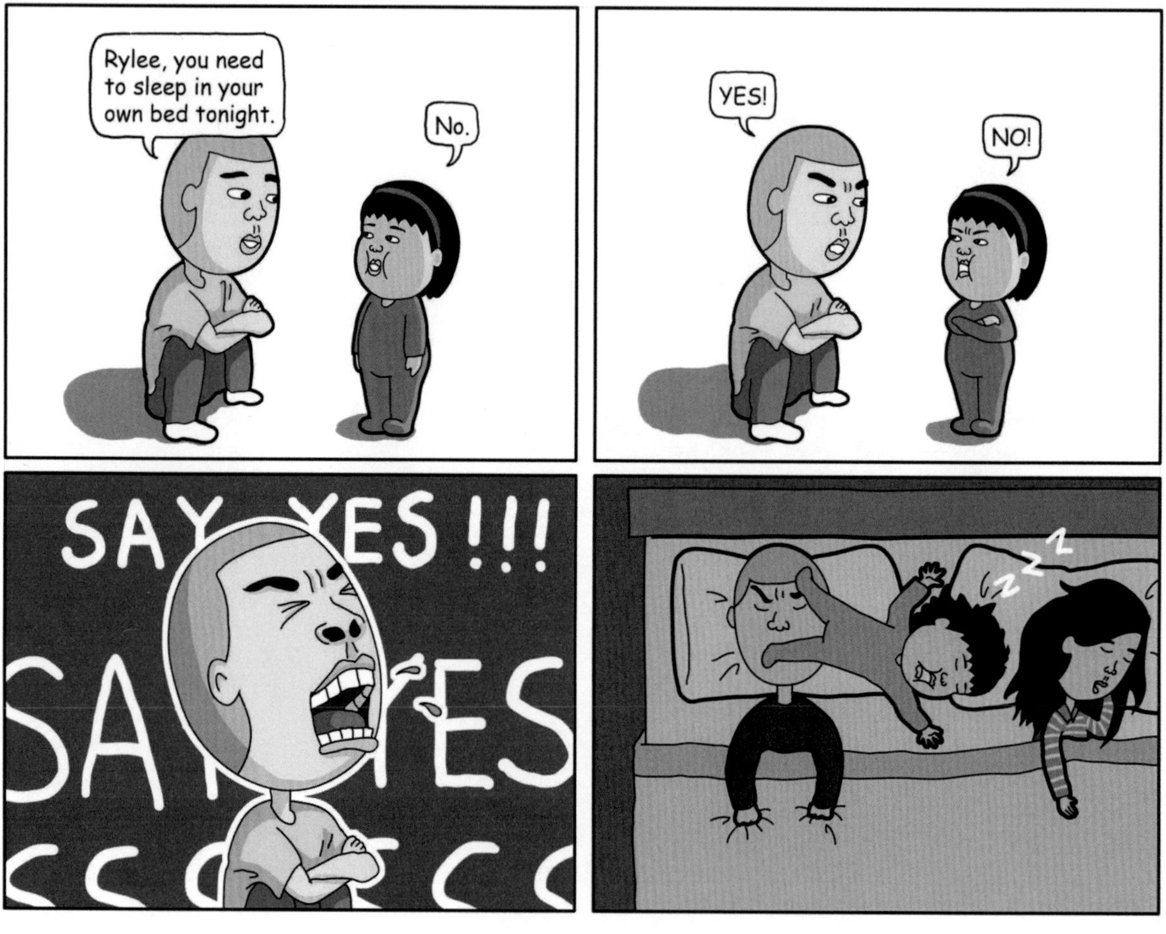
Rylee, you need to sleep in your own bed tonight.
No.
YES!
NO!
SAY YES!!!
Z Z Z

How did you start liking daddy?
He bought me ice cream.
LUCKYYY!!

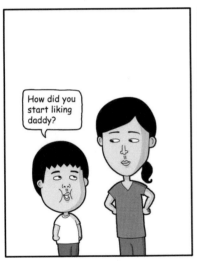

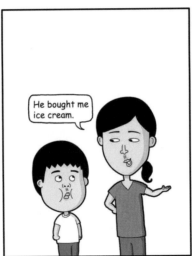

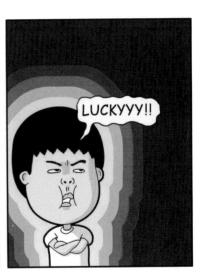

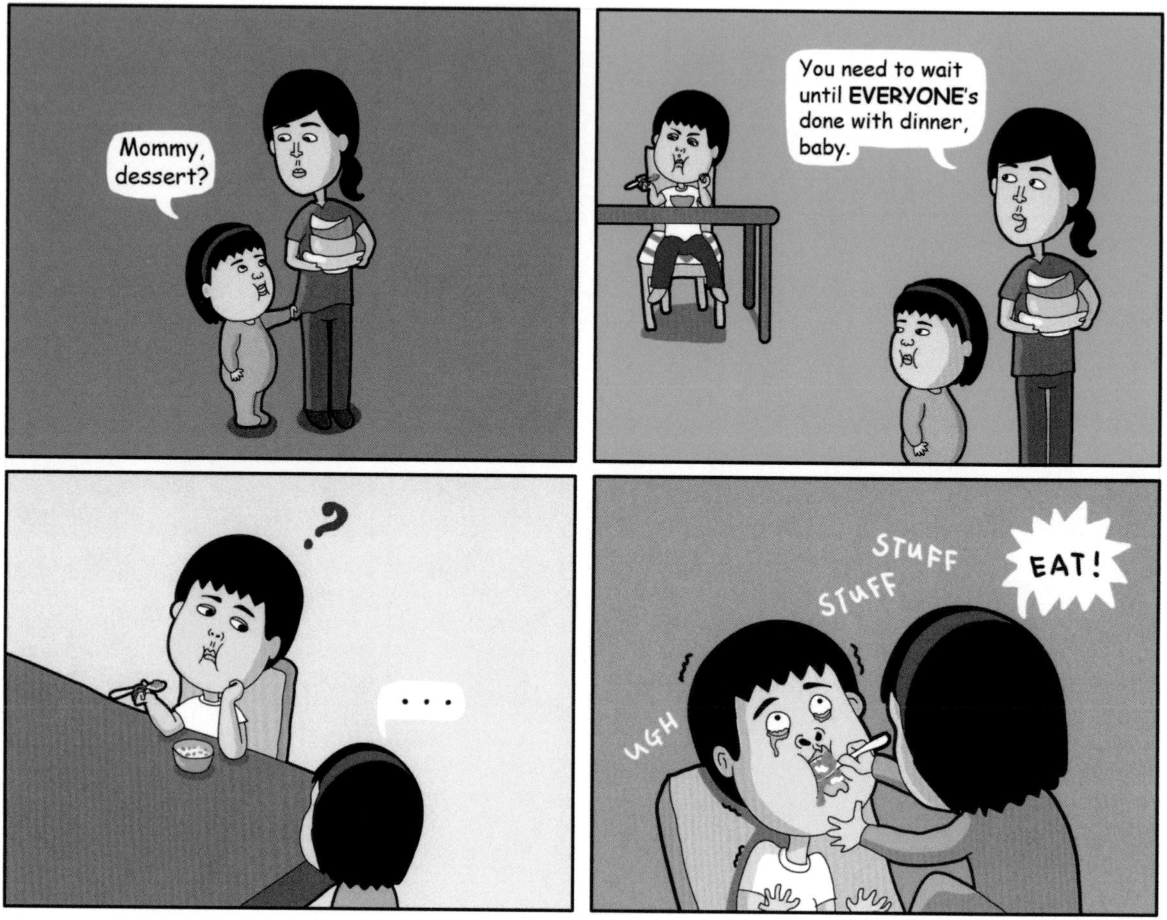
Mommy, dessert?
You need to wait until EVERYONE's done with dinner, baby.
?
...
STUFF
STUFF
EAT!
UGH

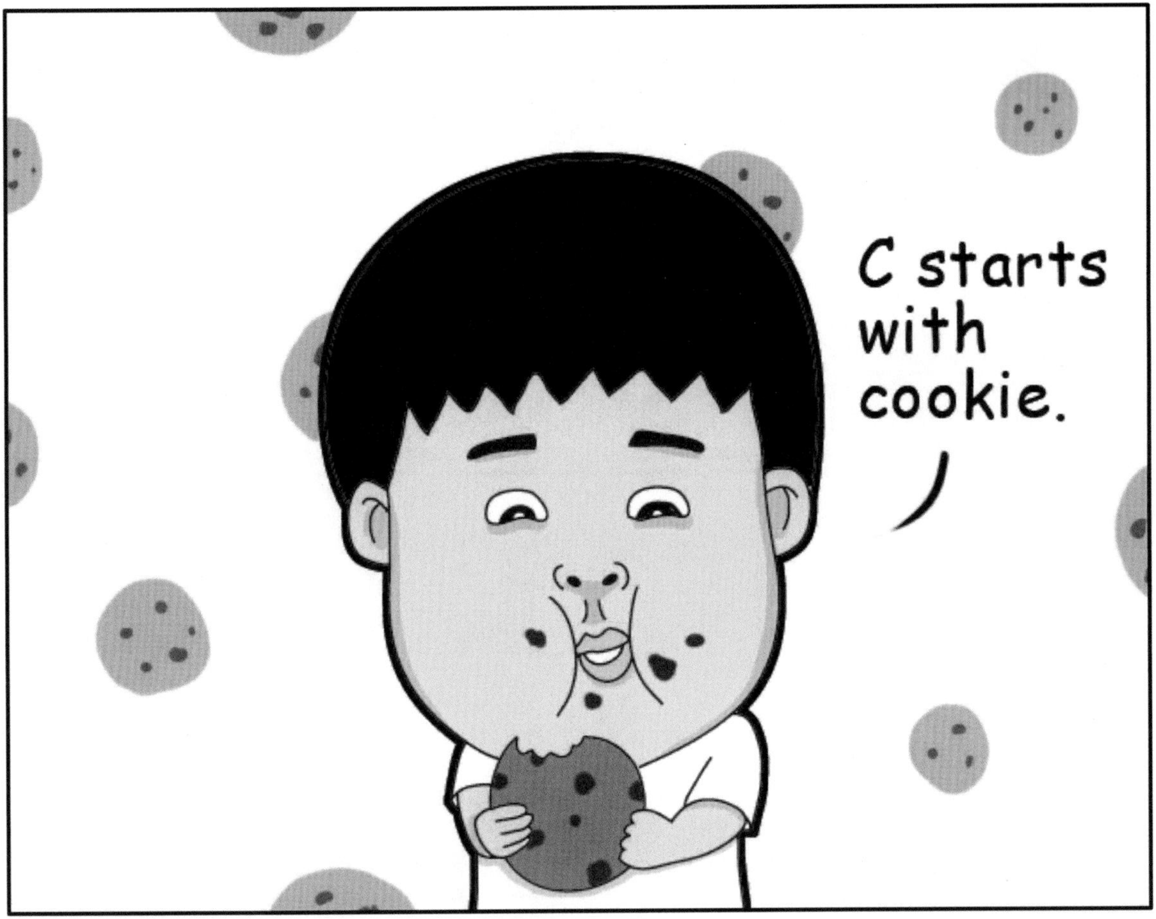
C starts with cookie.

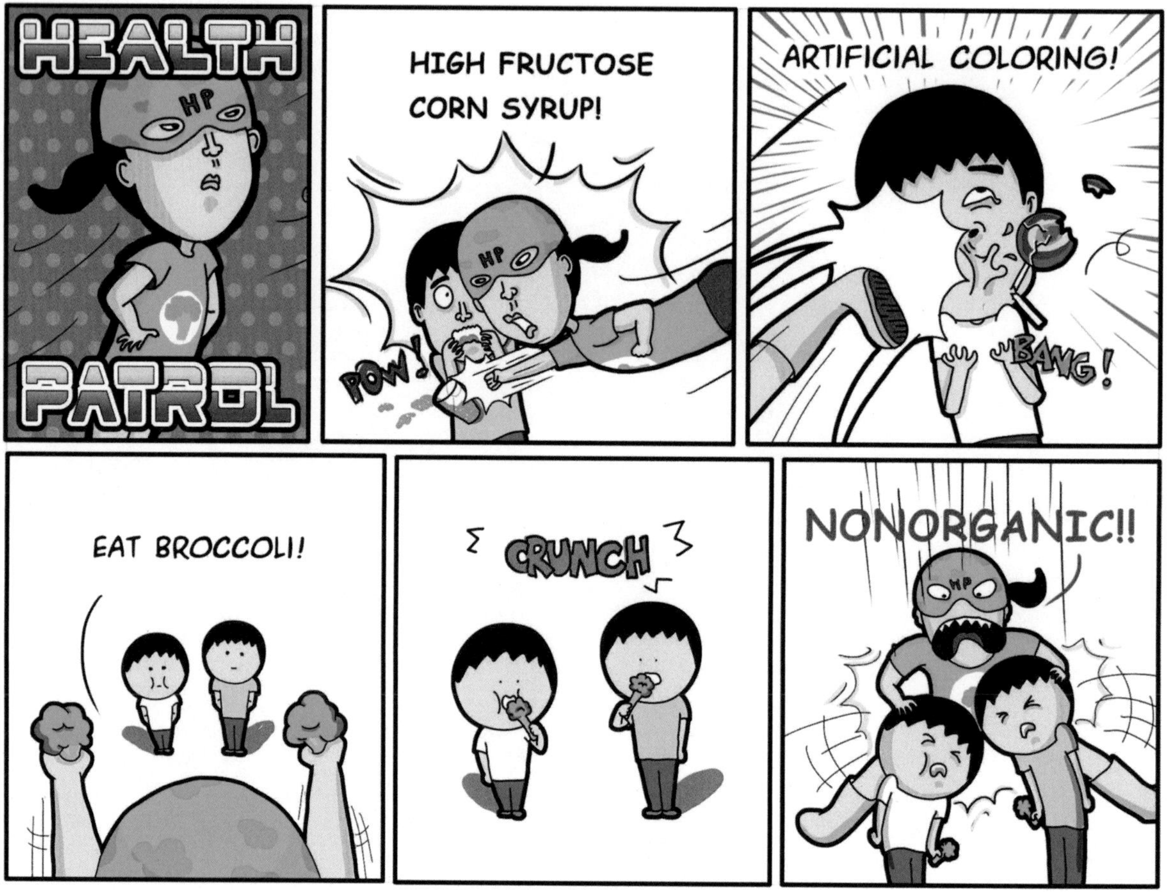
HEALTH
PATROL
HP
HIGH FRUCTOSE CORN SYRUP!
POW!
ARTIFICIAL COLORING!
BANG!
EAT BROCCOLI!
CRUNCH
NONORGANIC!!

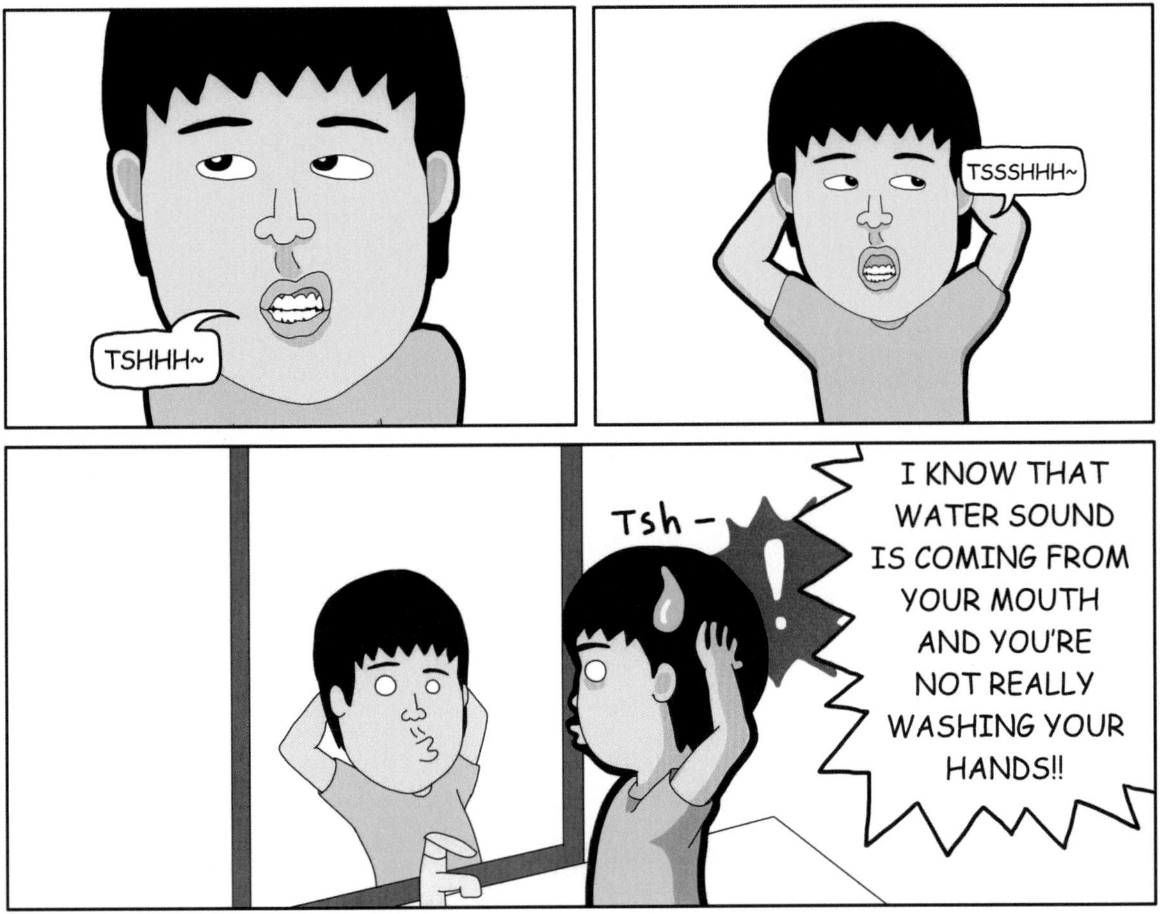
TSHHH~
TSSSHHH~
Tsh -
!
I KNOW THAT WATER SOUND IS COMING FROM YOUR MOUTH AND YOU'RE NOT REALLY WASHING YOUR HANDS!!

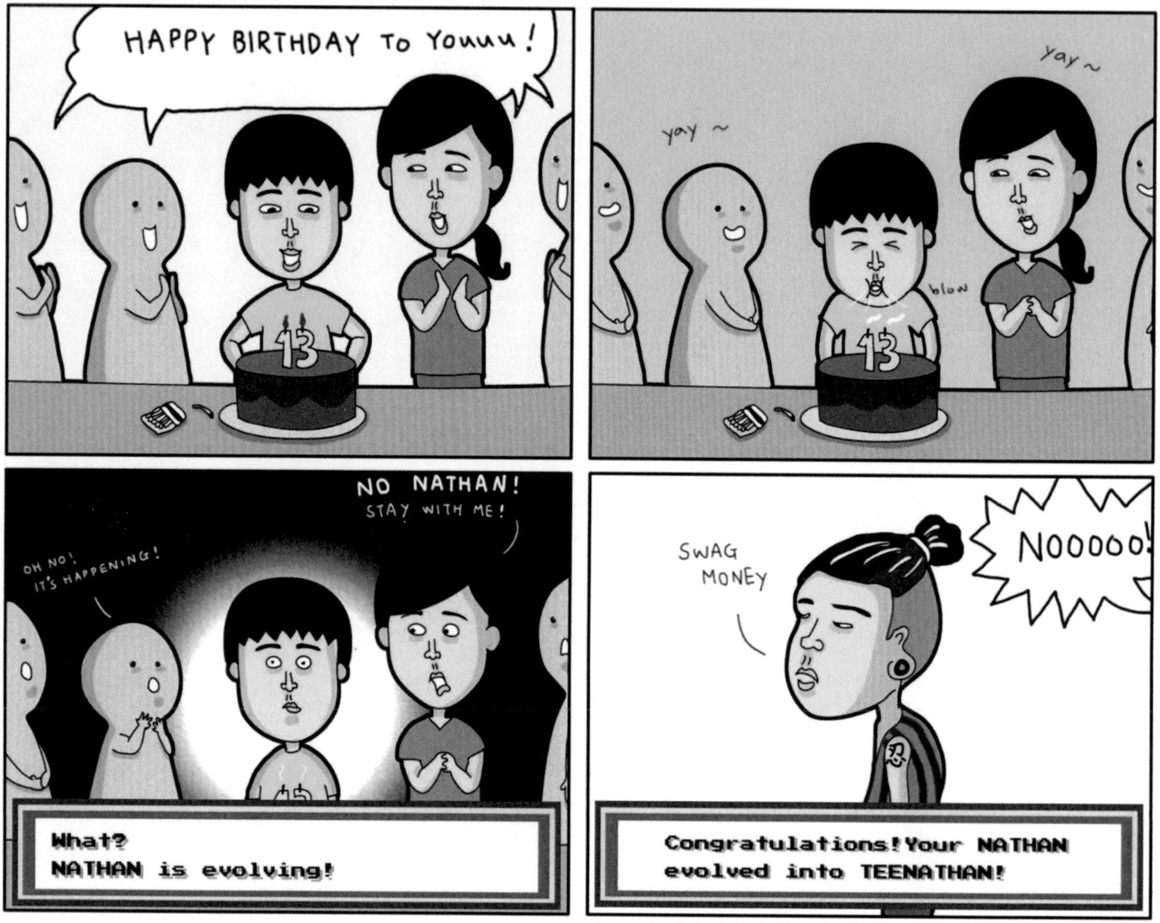
HAPPY BIRTHDAY TO Youuu!
yay ~
yay ~
blow
OH NO! IT'S HAPPENING!
NO NATHAN! STAY WITH ME!
What?
NATHAN is evolving!
SWAG MONEY
NOOOOO!
Congratulations! Your NATHAN evolved into TEENATHAN!

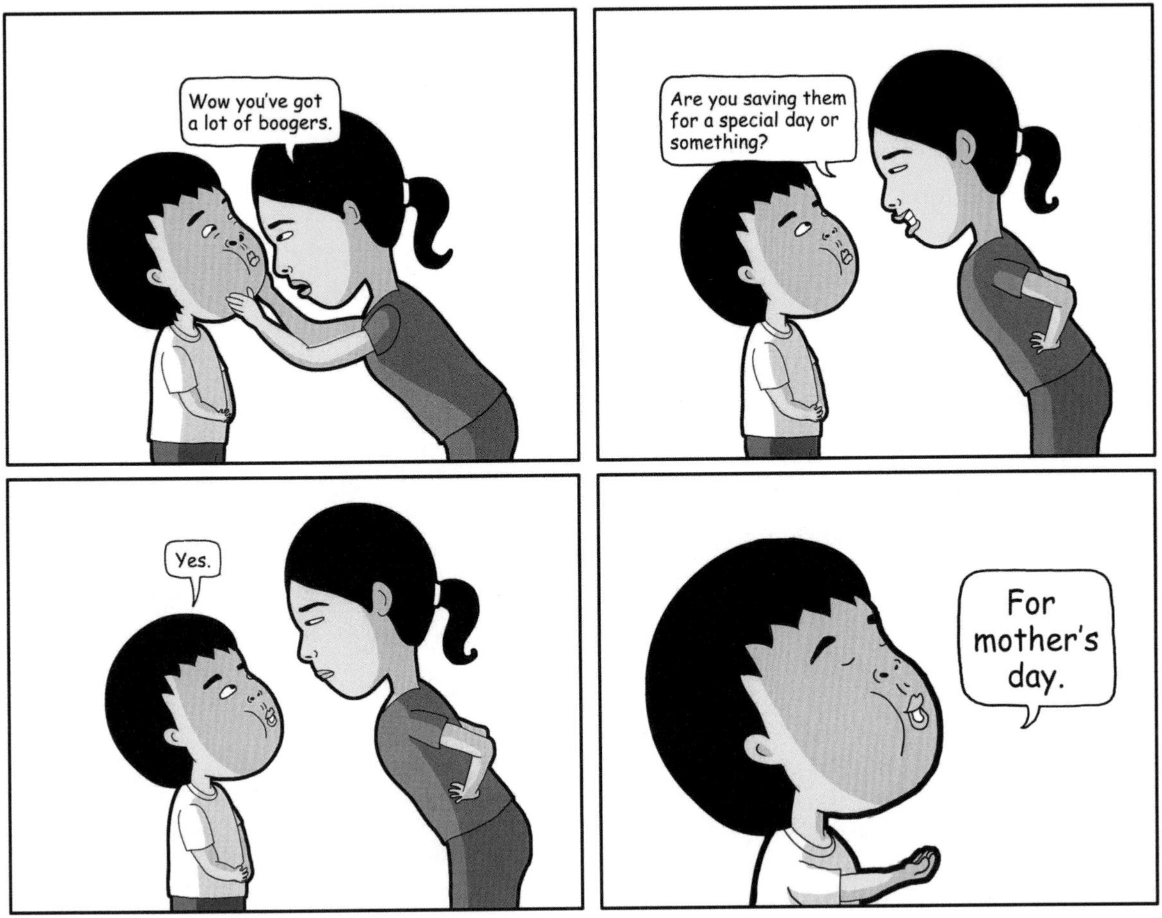
Wow you've got a lot of boogers.
Are you saving them for a special day or something?
Yes.
For mother's day.

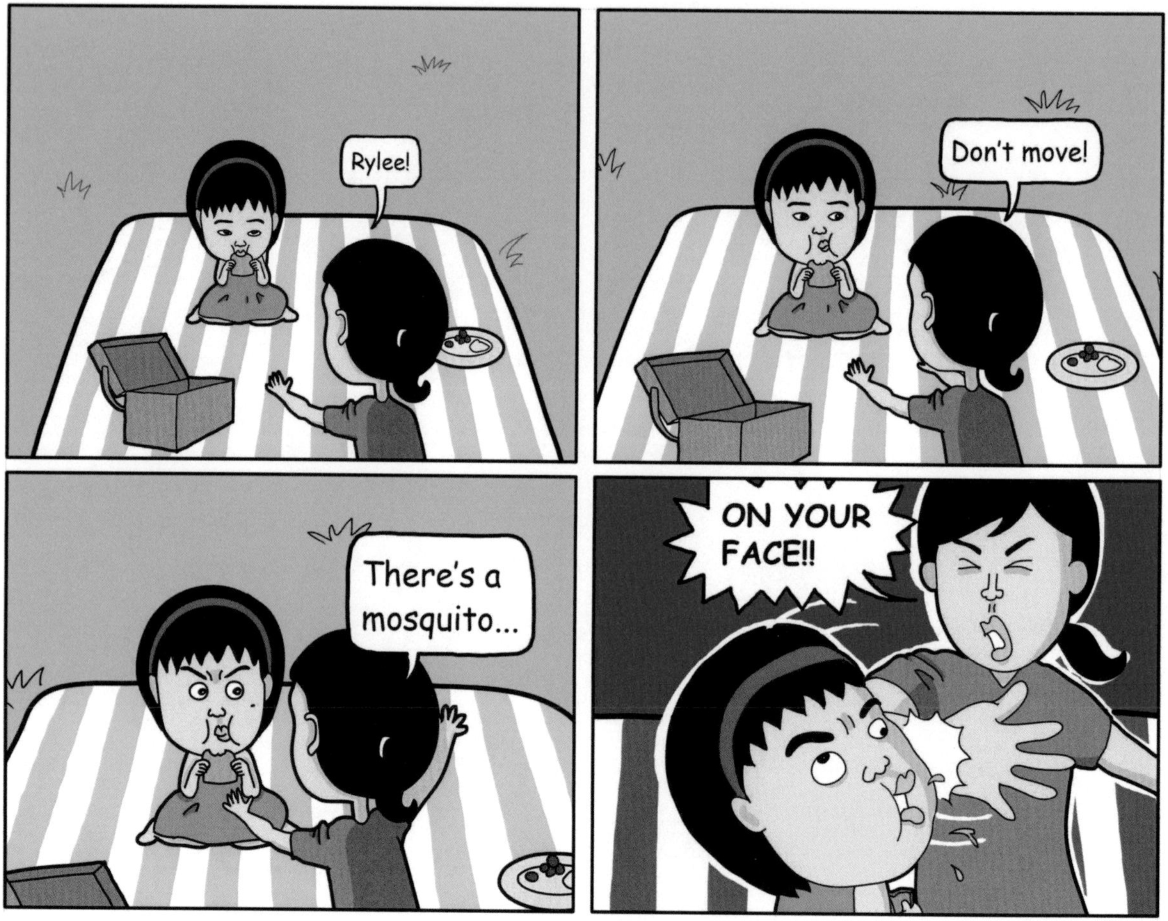
Rylee!
Don't move!
There's a mosquito...
ON YOUR FACE!!

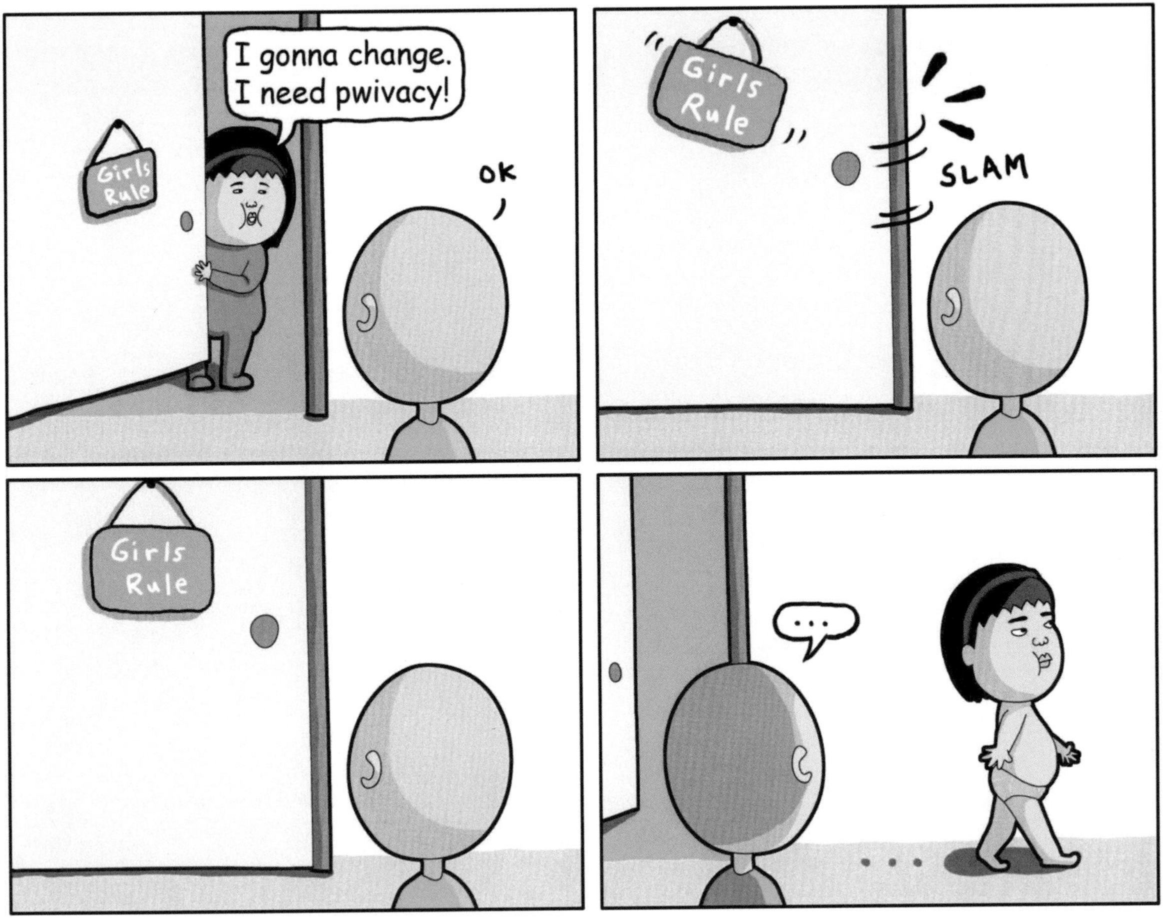
I gonna change. I need pwivacy!
OK
Girls Rule
SLAM
...

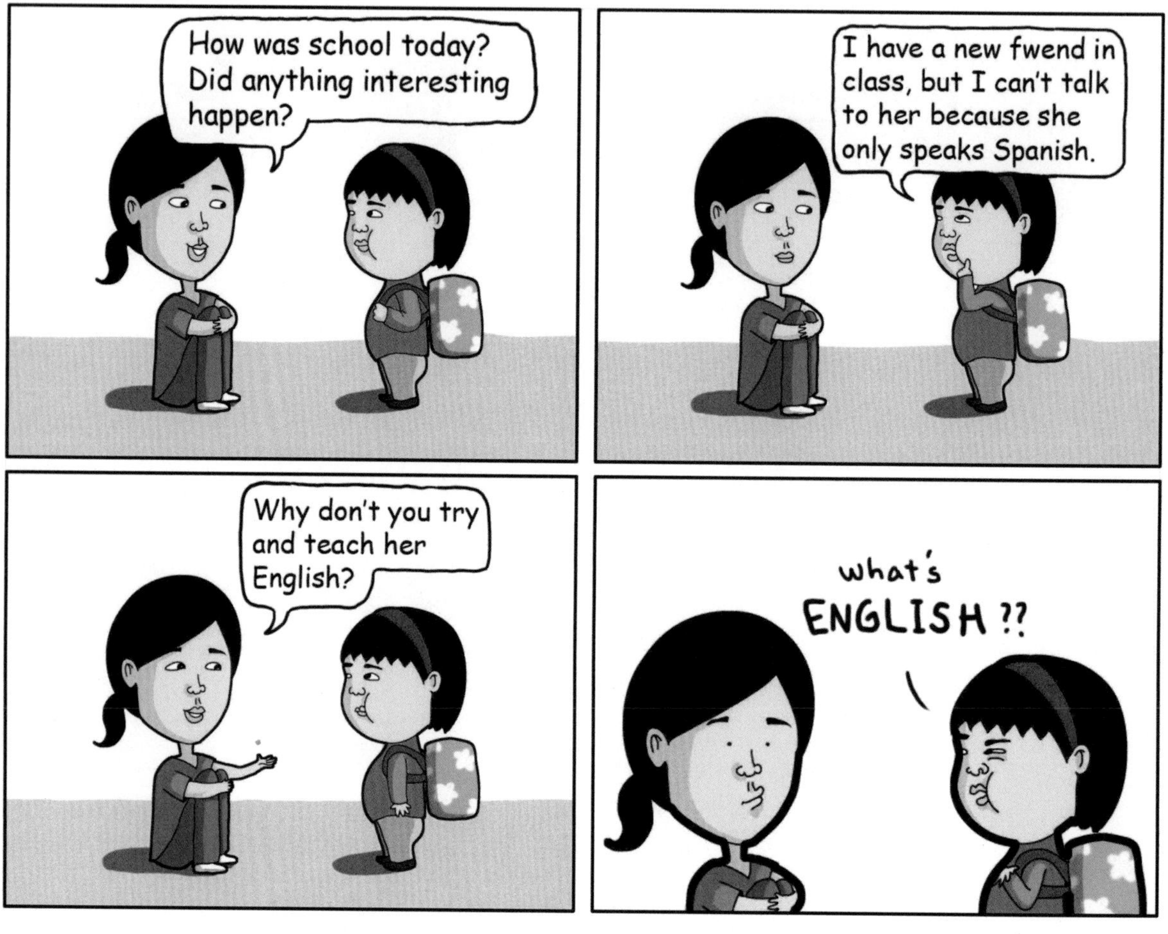
How was school today? Did anything interesting happen?
I have a new fwend in class, but I can't talk to her because she only speaks Spanish.
Why don't you try and teach her English?
what's ENGLISH ??

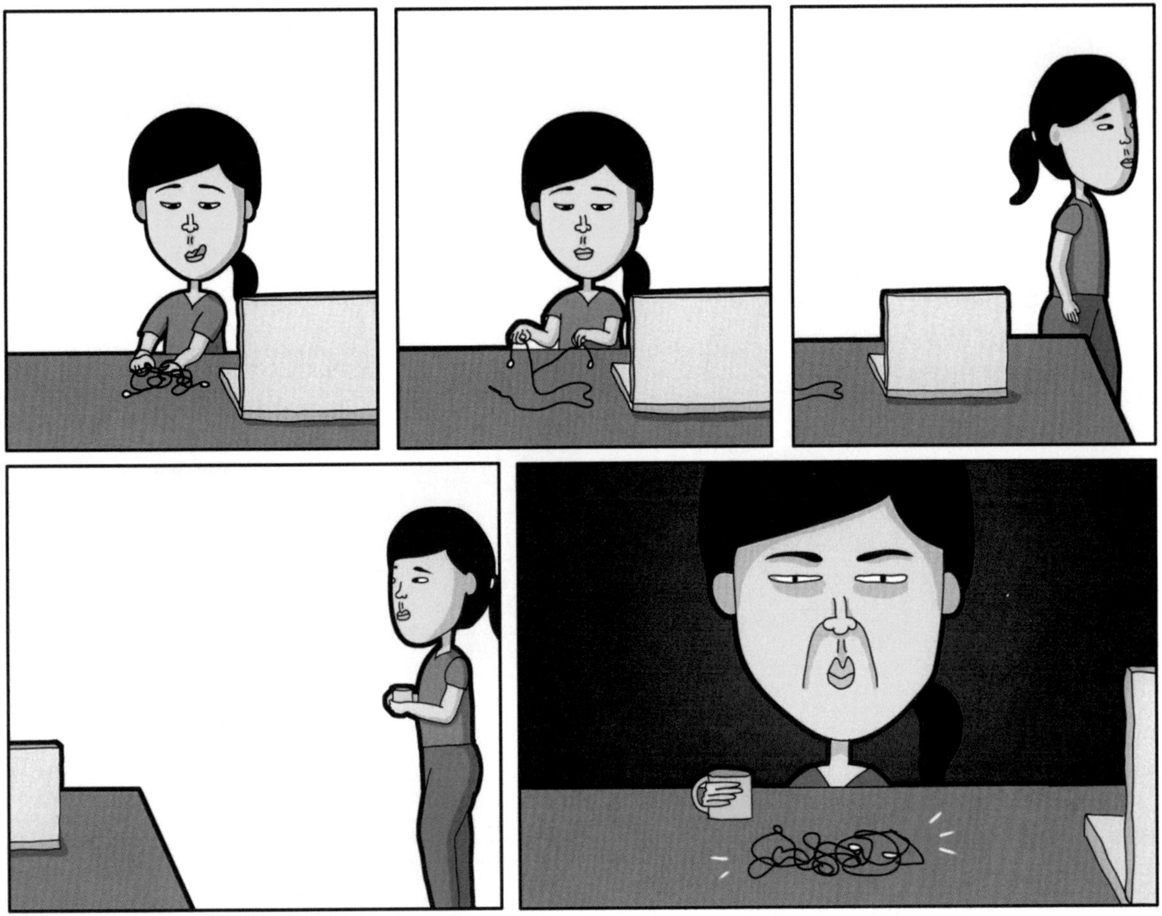

Rylee, I said no more chips.
JUST. DON'T. LOOK AT ME!!!

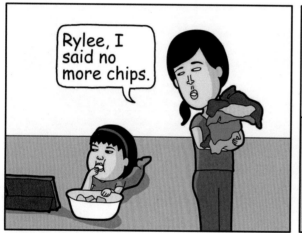

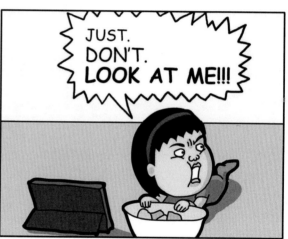

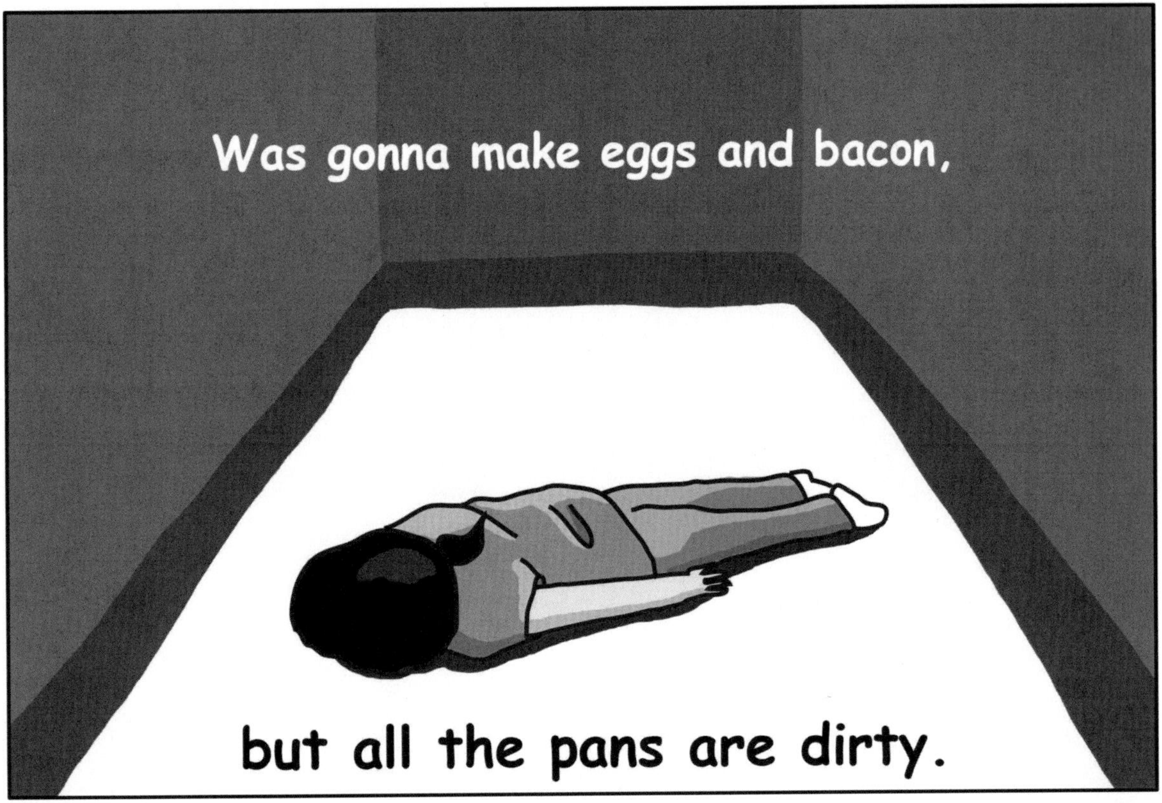
Was gonna make eggs and bacon,
but all the pans are dirty.

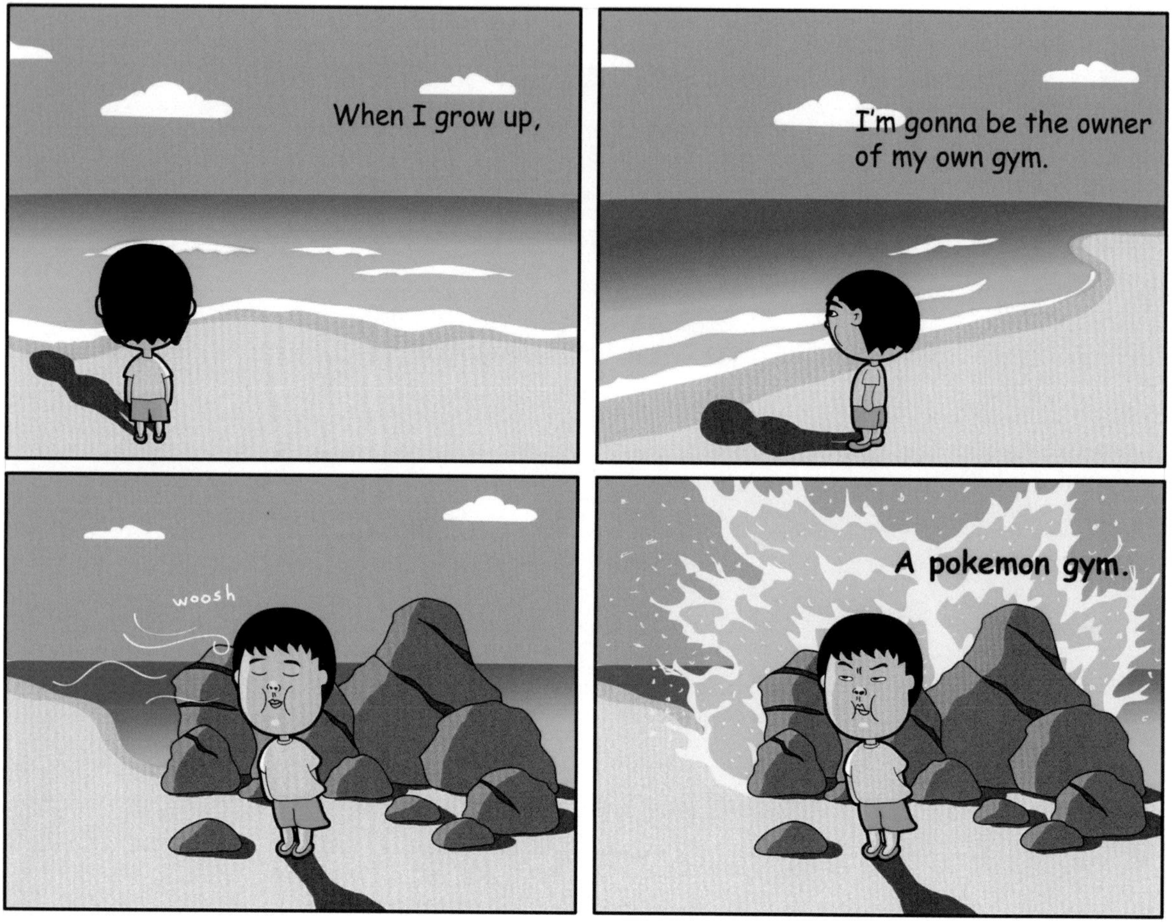
When I grow up,
I'm gonna be the owner of my own gym.
woosh
A pokemon gym.

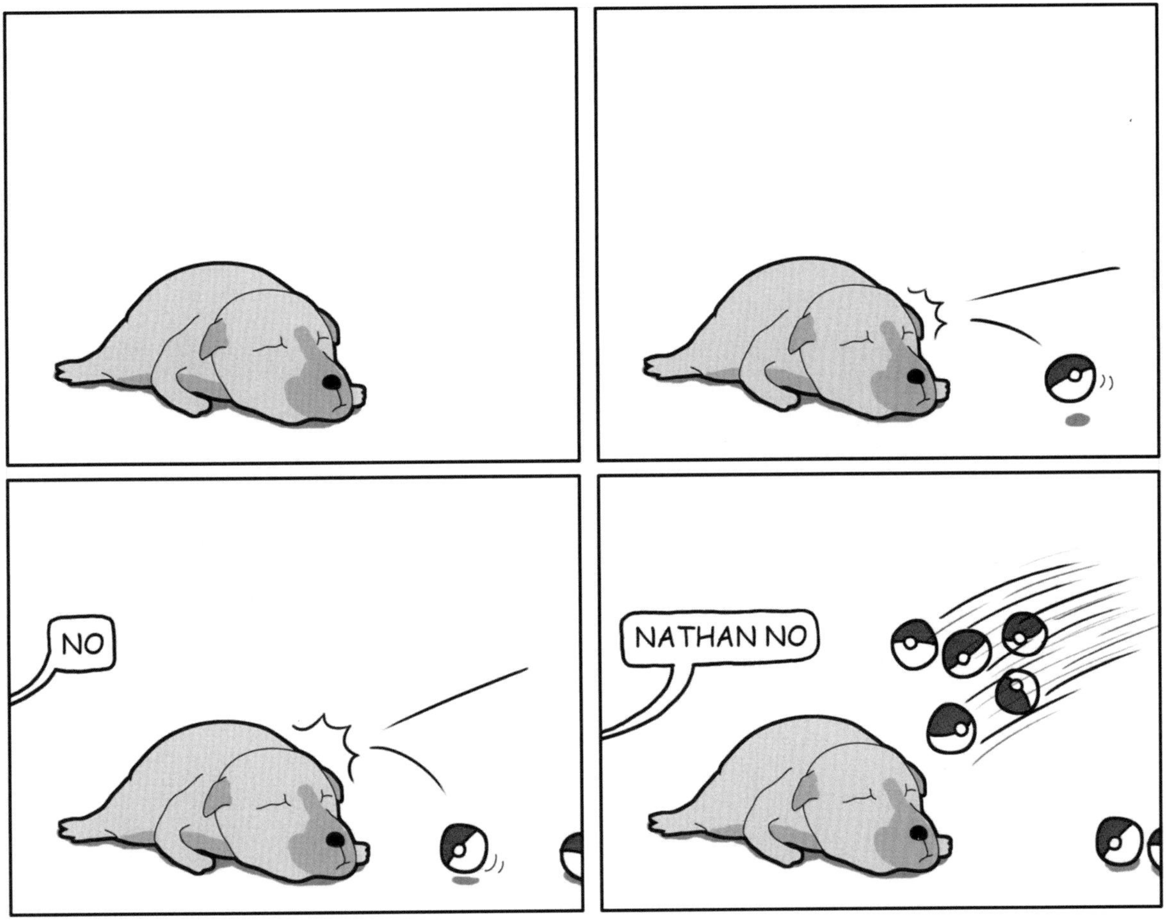
NO
NATHAN NO

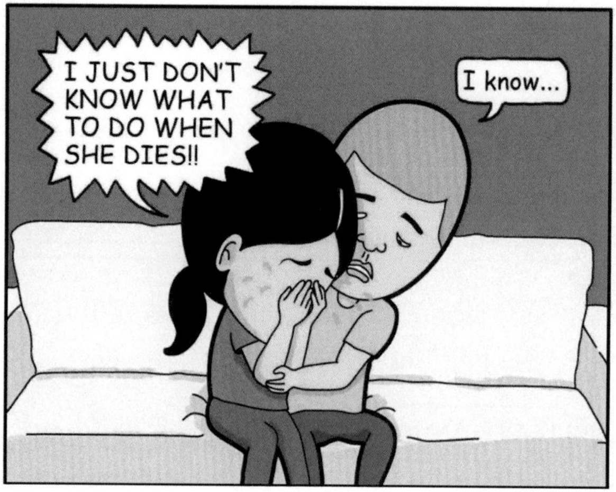
I JUST DON'T KNOW WHAT TO DO WHEN SHE DIES!!
I know...

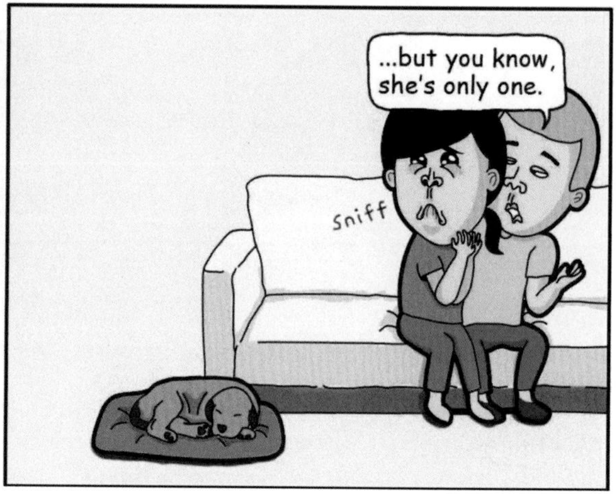
...but you know, she's only one.
Sniff

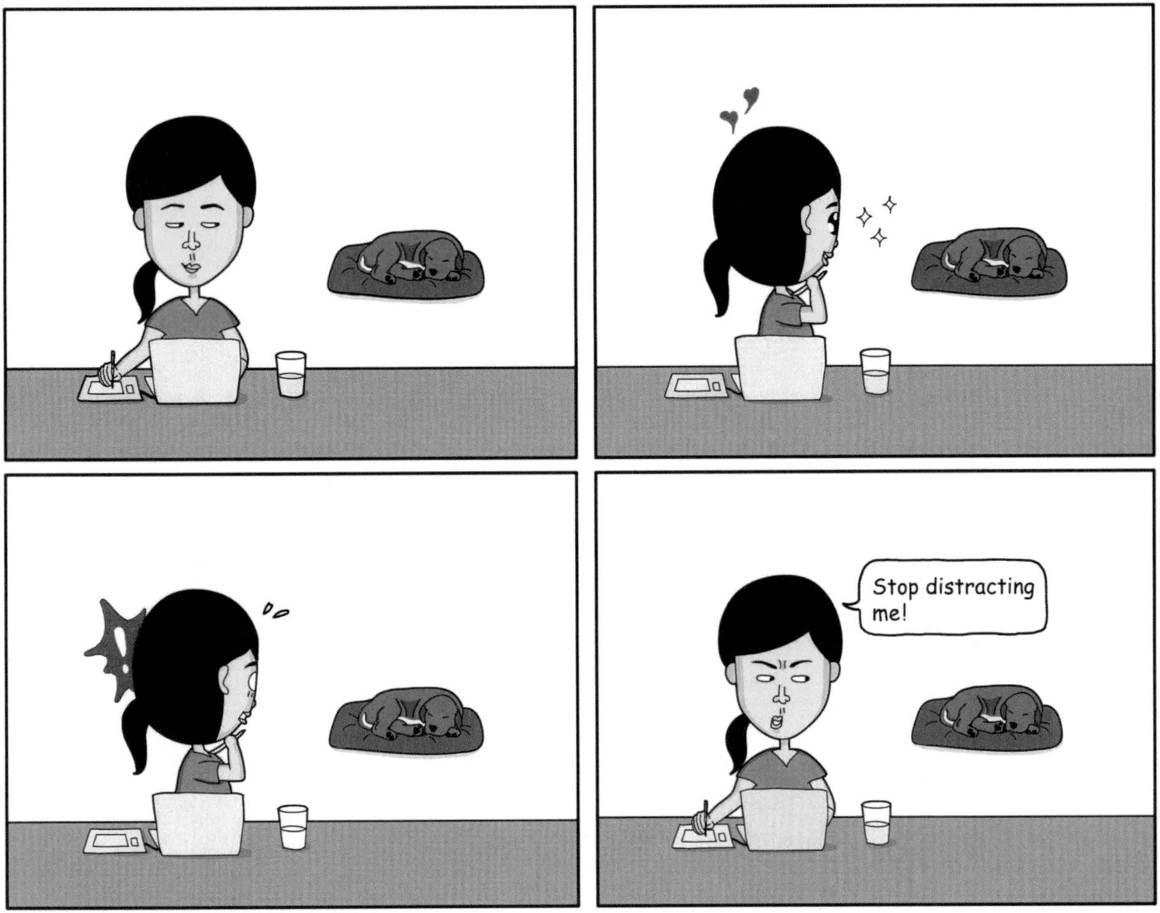
Stop distracting me!

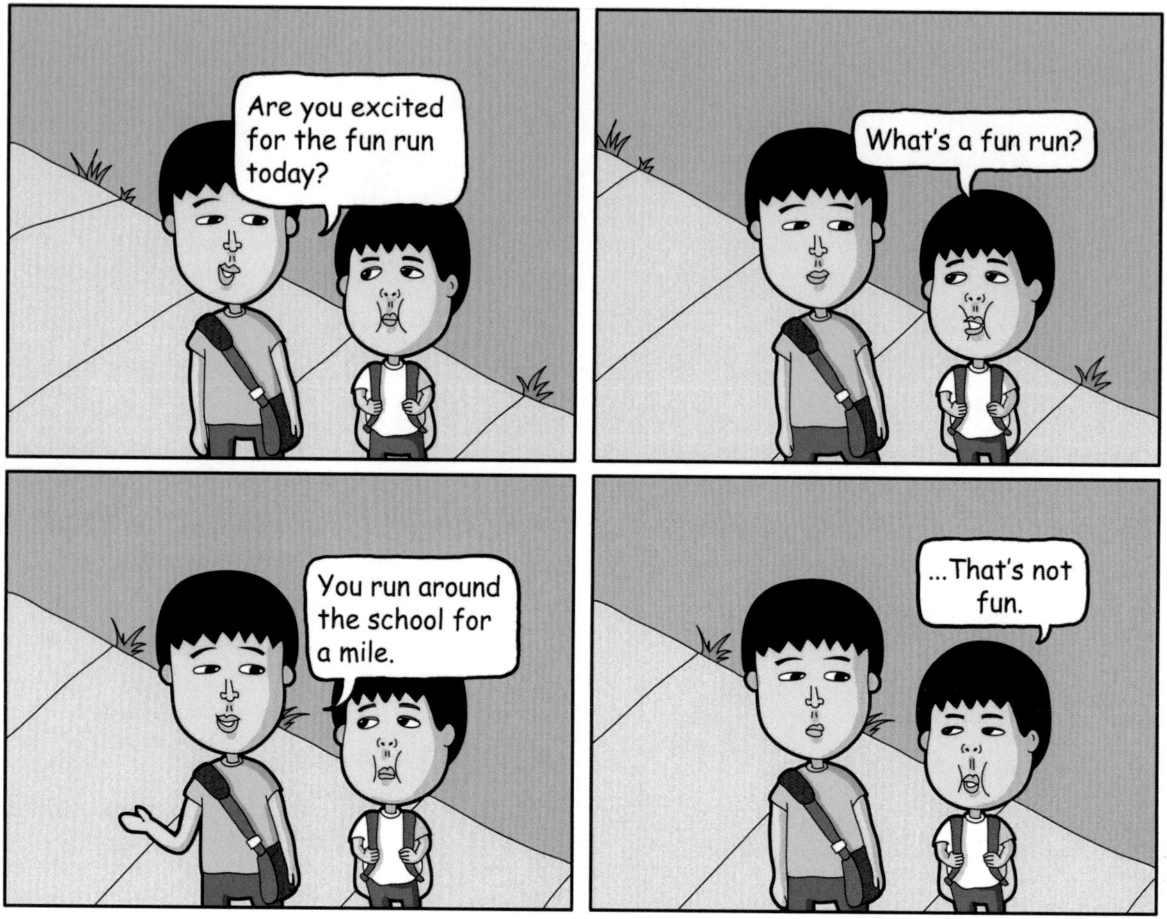
Are you excited for the fun run today?
What's a fun run?
You run around the school for a mile.
...That's not fun.

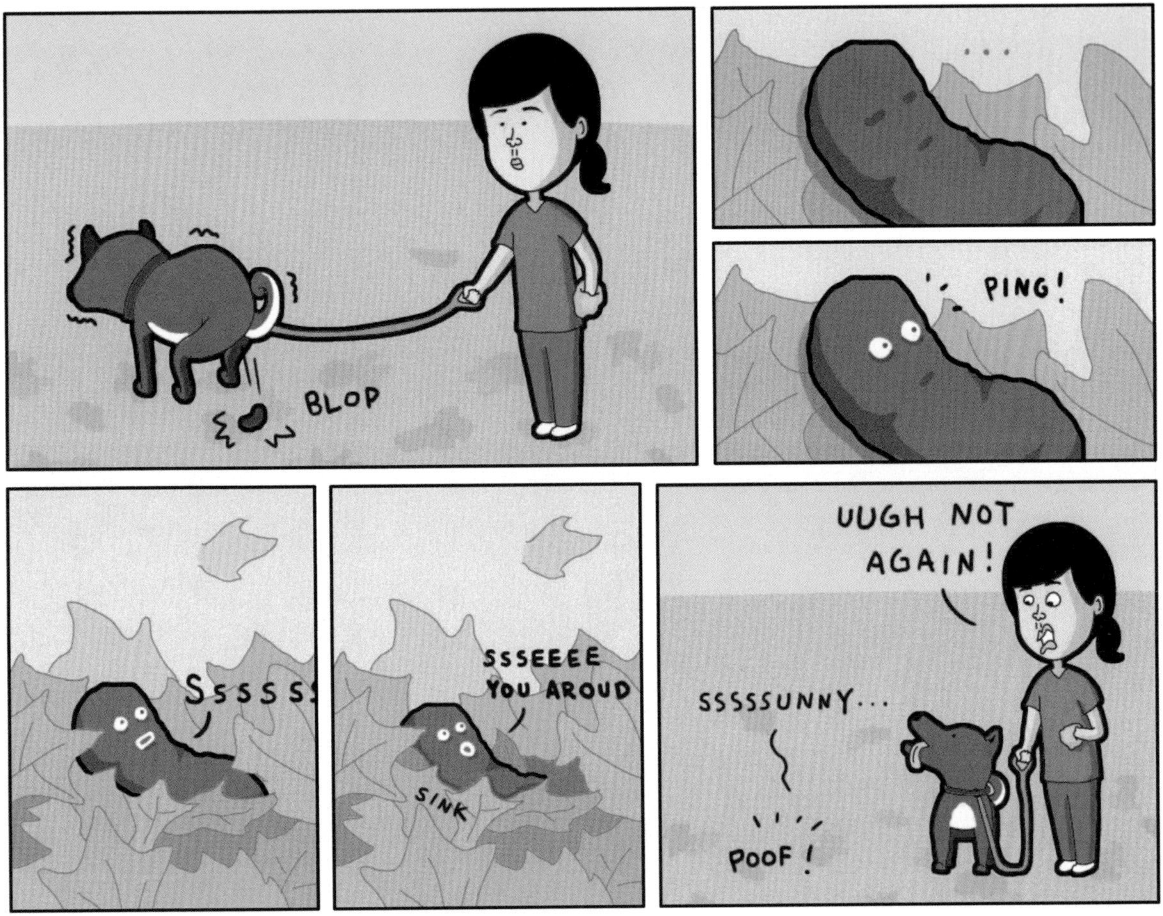
BLOP
...
PING!
SSSSSS
SSSEEEE YOU AROUD
SINK
UUGH NOT AGAIN!
SSSSSUNNY...
POOF!

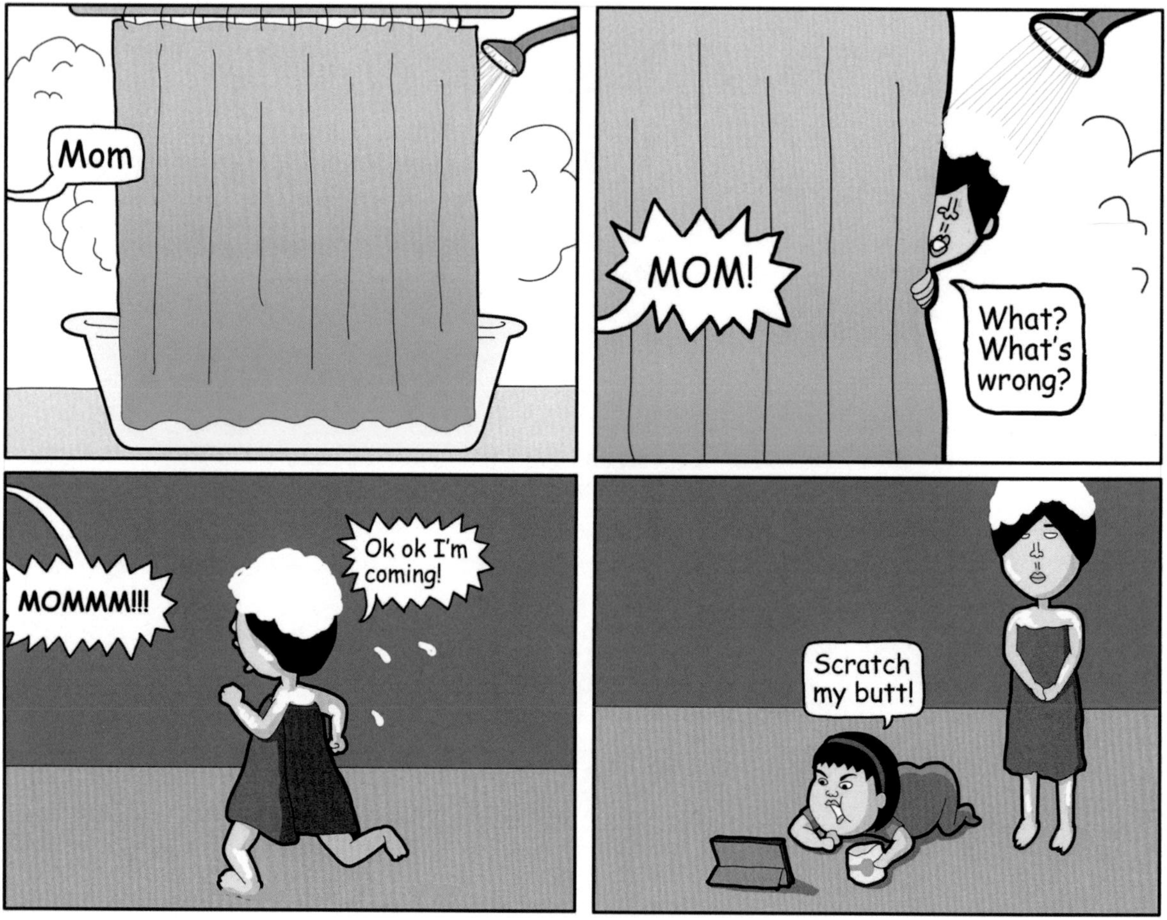
Mom
MOM!
What? What's wrong?
MOMMM!!!
Ok ok I'm coming!
Scratch my butt!

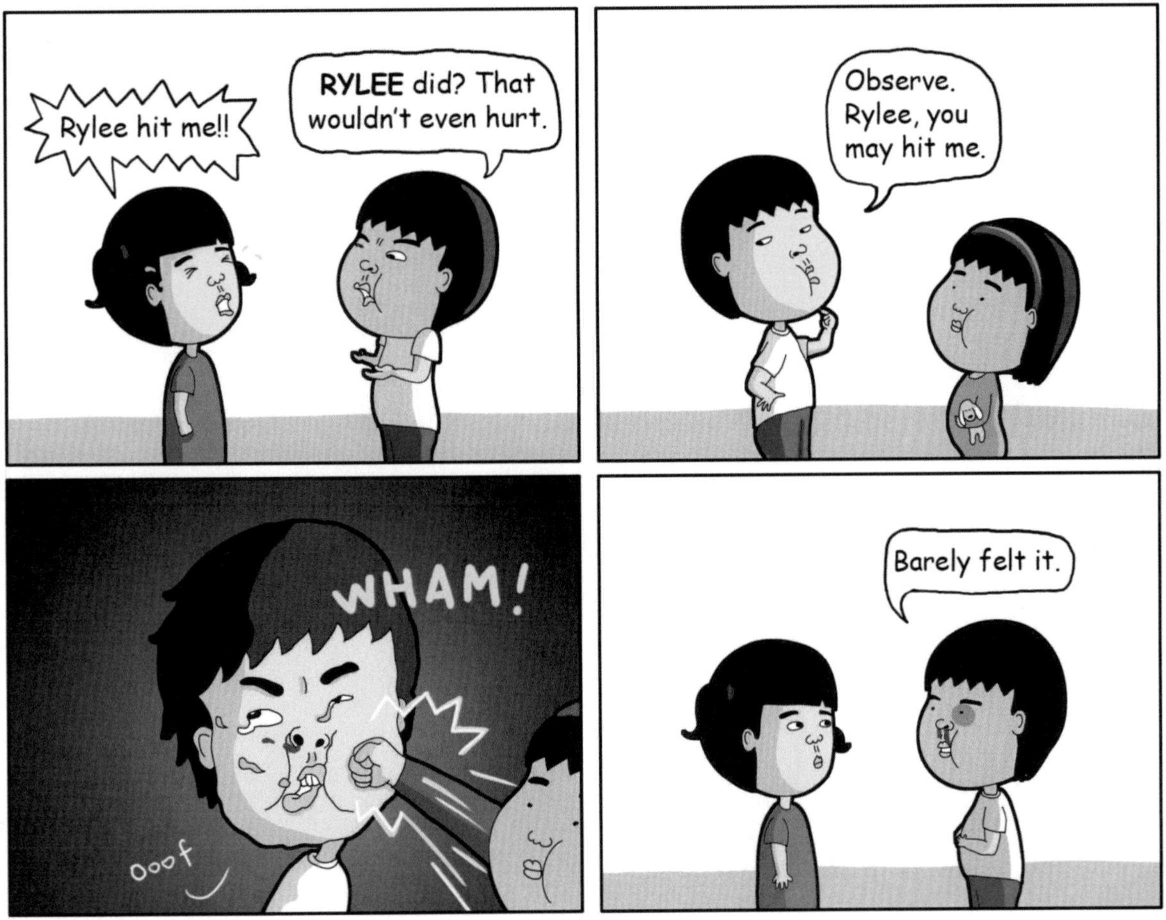
Rylee hit me!!
RYLEE did? That wouldn't even hurt.
Observe. Rylee, you may hit me.
WHAM!
Ooof
Barely felt it.

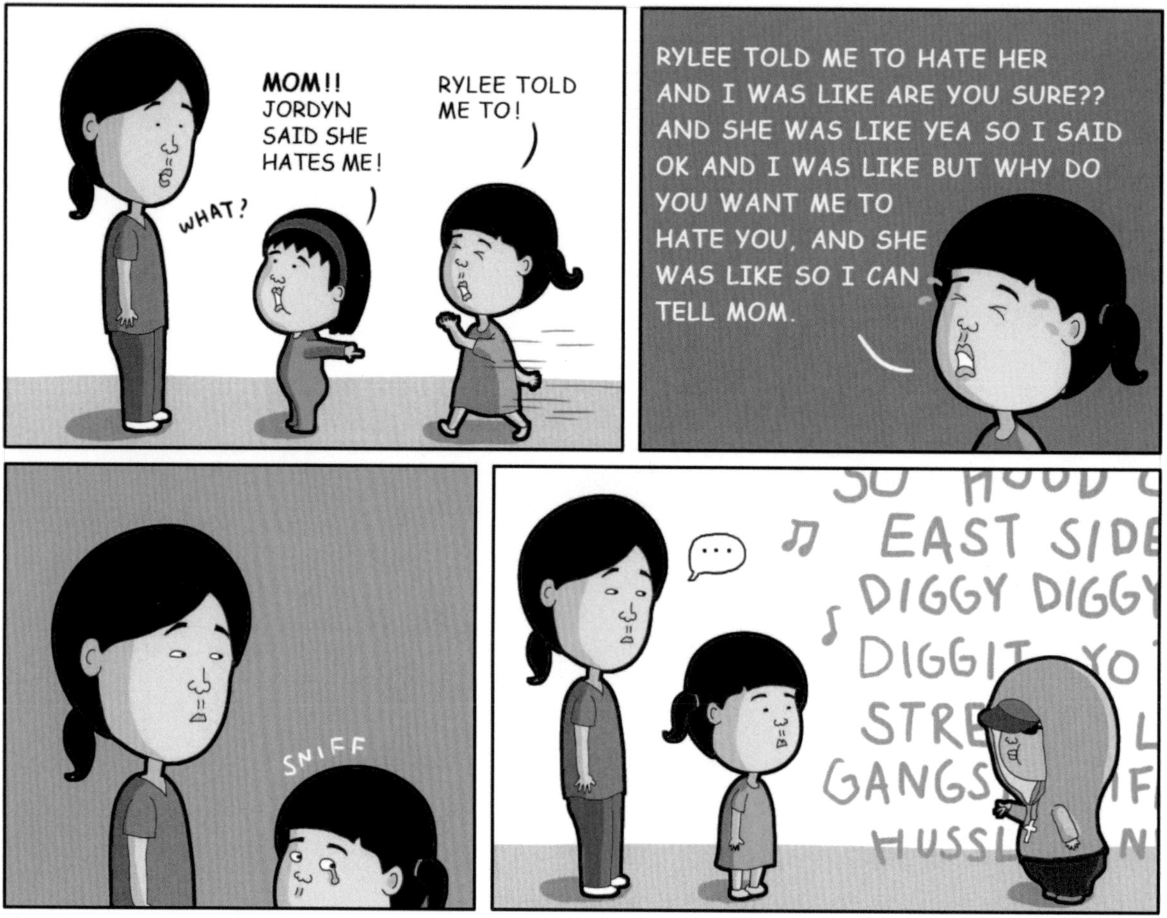

MOM!! JORDYN SAID SHE HATES ME!
RYLEE TOLD ME TO!
WHAT?
RYLEE TOLD ME TO HATE HER AND I WAS LIKE ARE YOU SURE?? AND SHE WAS LIKE YEA SO I SAID OK AND I WAS LIKE BUT WHY DO YOU WANT ME TO HATE YOU, AND SHE WAS LIKE SO I CAN TELL MOM.
SNIFF
...
EAST SIDE
DIGGY DIGGY
DIGGIT YO
GANGS

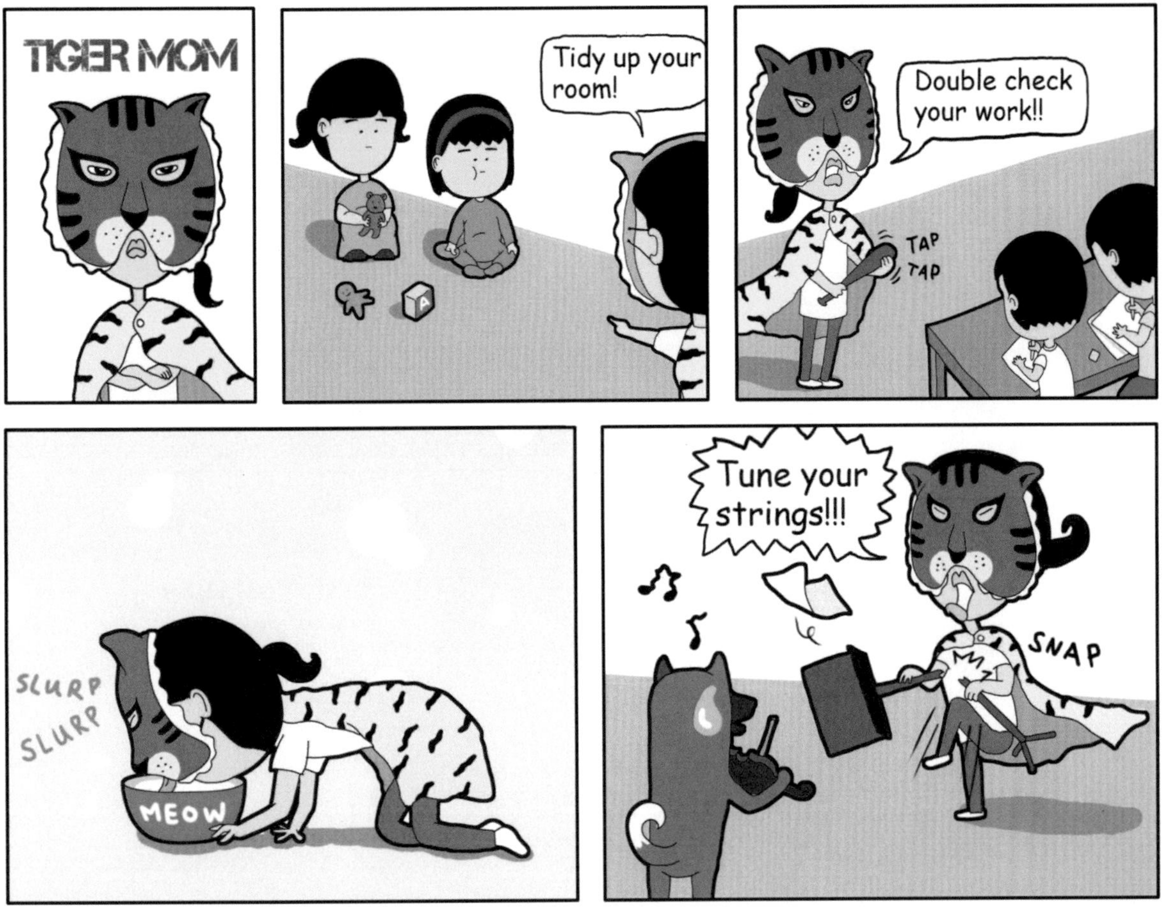
TIGER MOM
Tidy up your room!
Double check your work!!
TAP
TAP
SLURP
SLURP
MEOW
Tune your strings!!!
SNAP

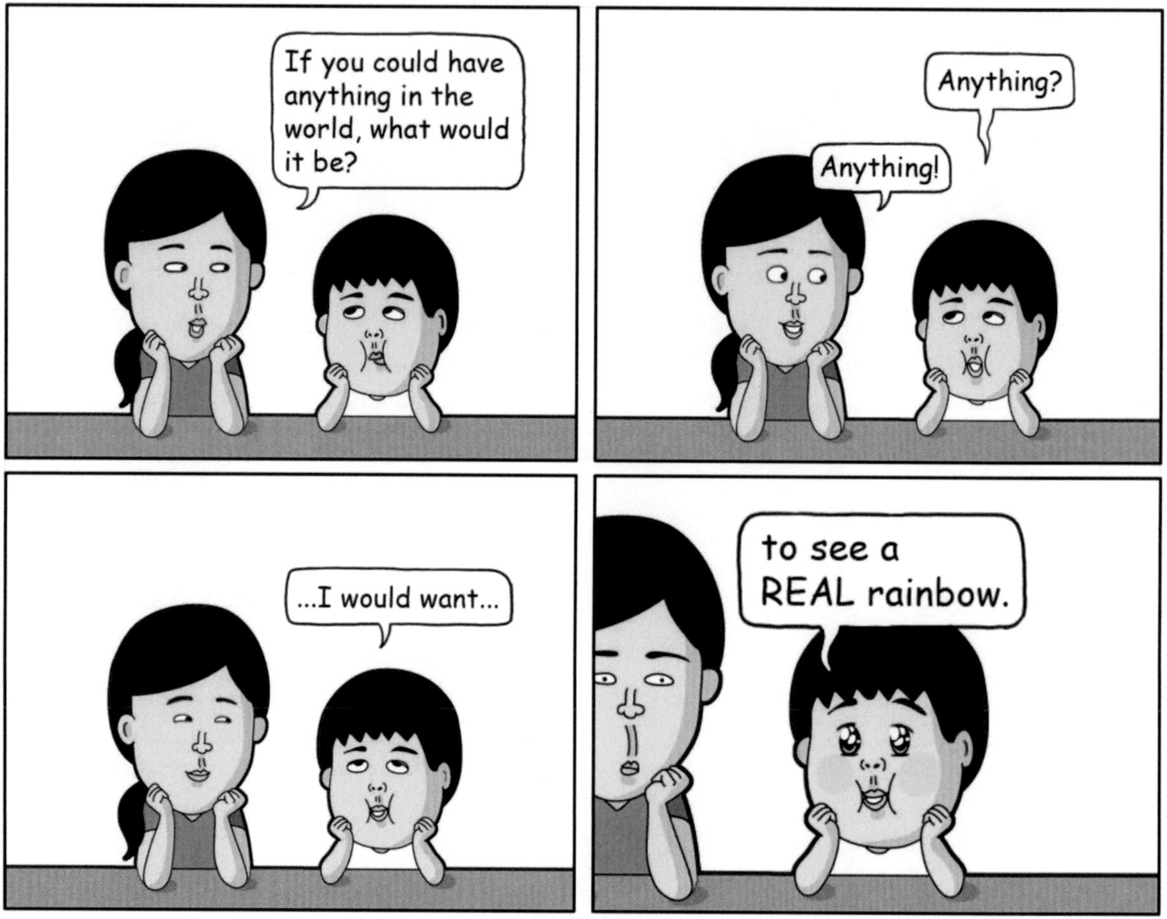
If you could have anything in the world, what would it be?
Anything?
Anything!
...I would want...
to see a REAL rainbow.

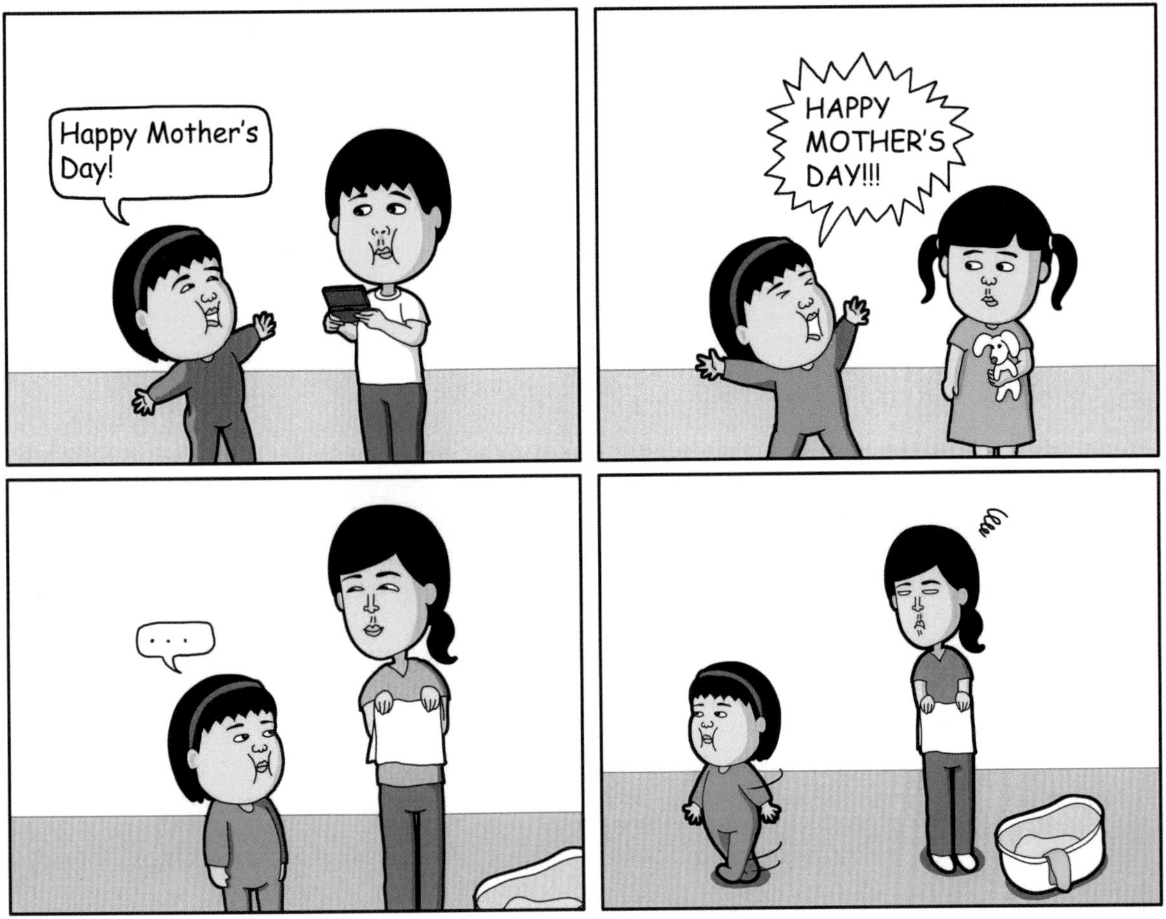
Happy Mother's Day!
HAPPY MOTHER'S DAY!!!
. . .

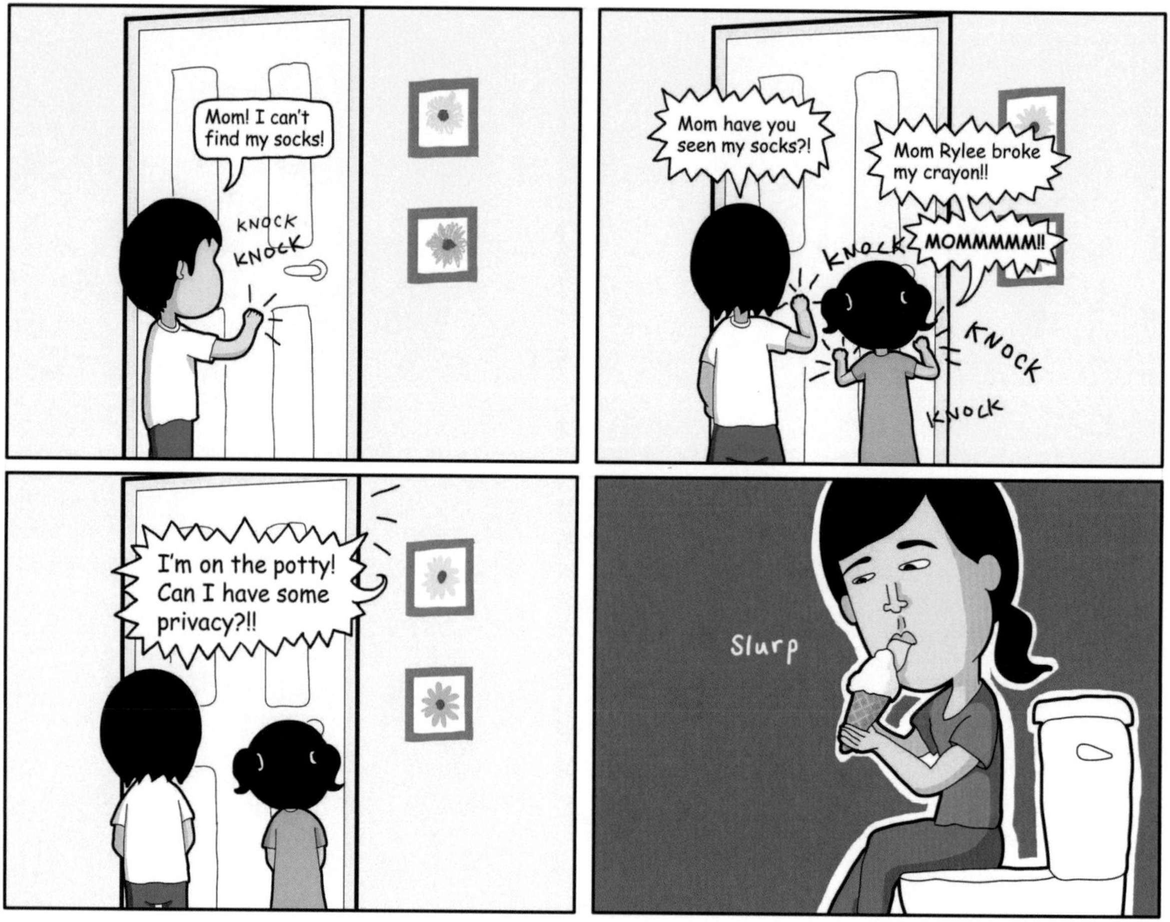
Mom! I can't find my socks!
KNOCK
KNOCK
Mom have you seen my socks?!
Mom Rylee broke my crayon!!
KNOCK
MOMMMMM!!
KNOCK
KNOCK
I'm on the potty! Can I have some privacy?!!
Slurp

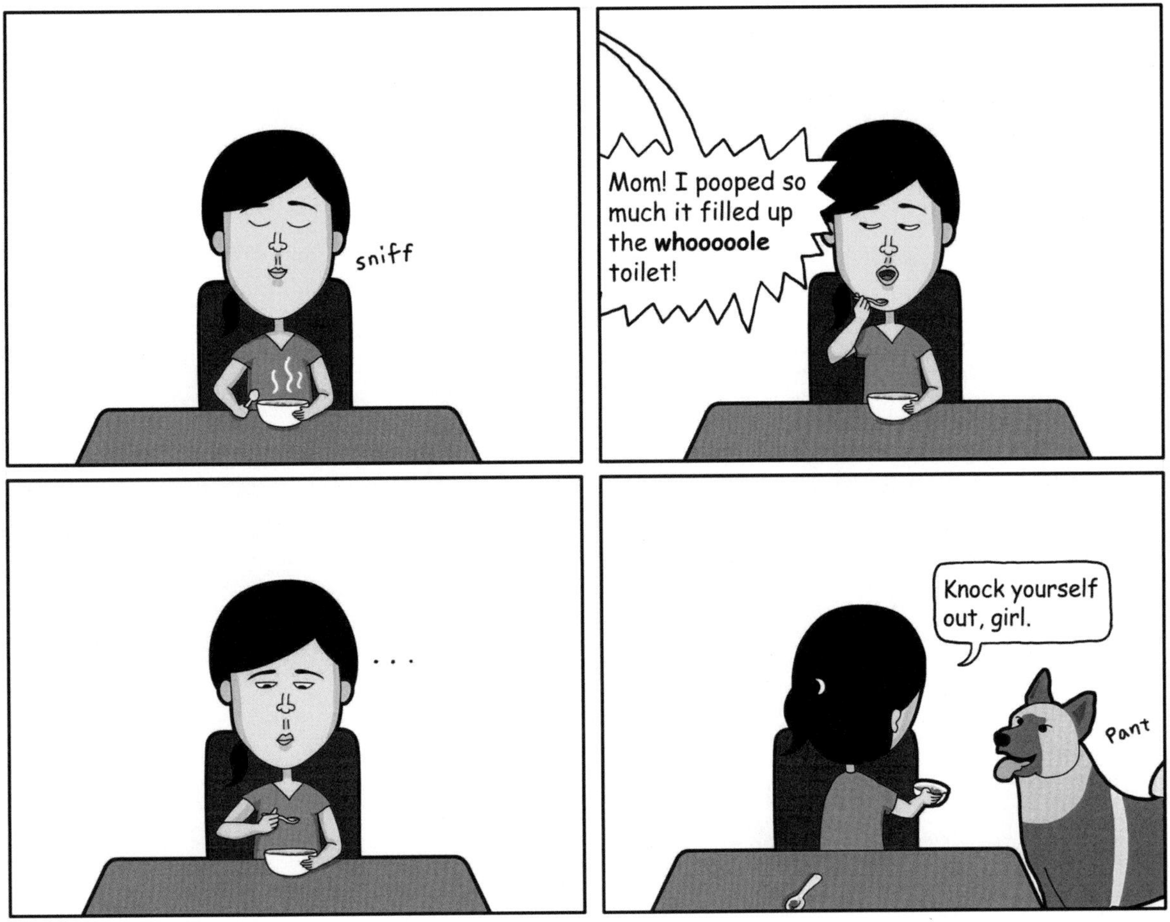
sniff
Mom! I pooped so much it filled up the **whooooole** toilet!
. . .
Knock yourself out, girl.
Pant

Money can't buy happiness
BUT IT CAN BUY PIZZA

AND THAT'S PRETTY MUCH THE SAME THING

- source unknown

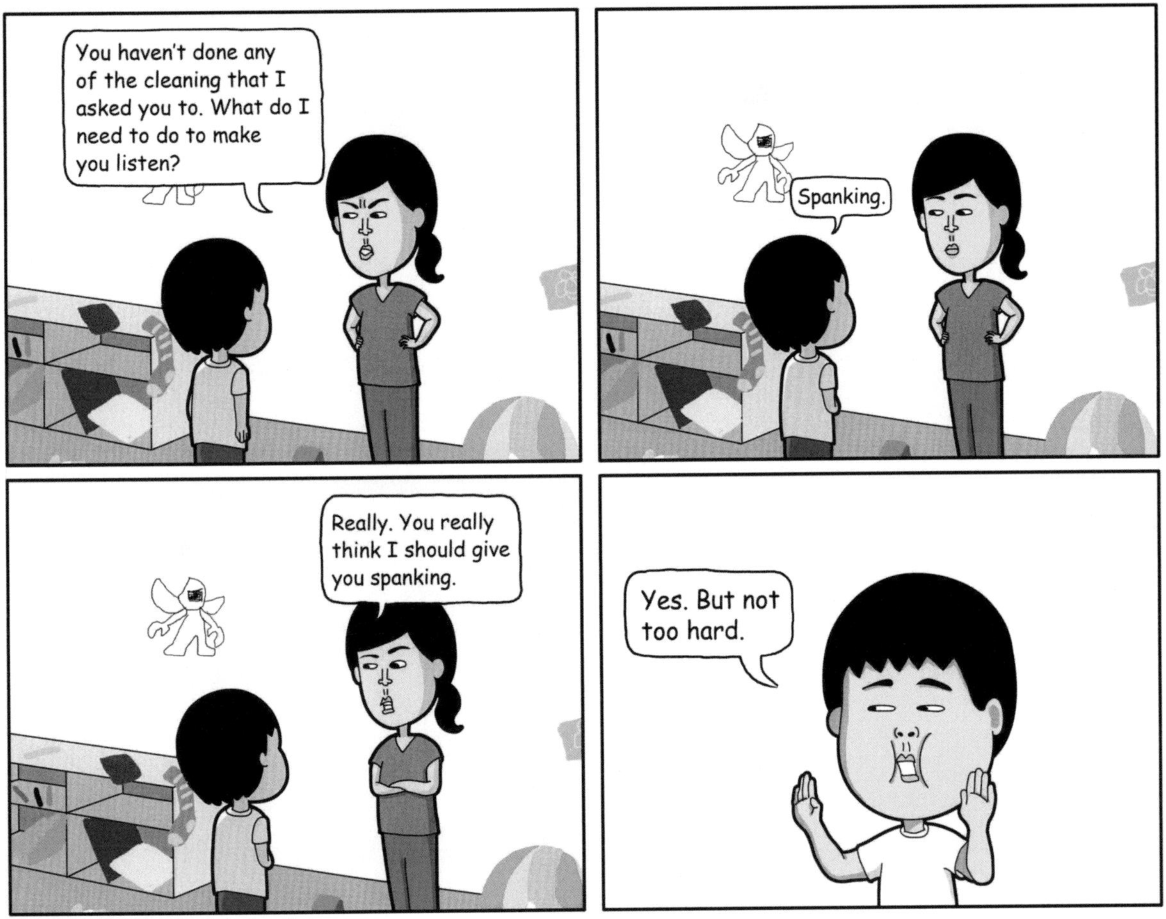
You haven't done any of the cleaning that I asked you to. What do I need to do to make you listen?
Spanking.
Really. You really think I should give you spanking.
Yes. But not too hard.

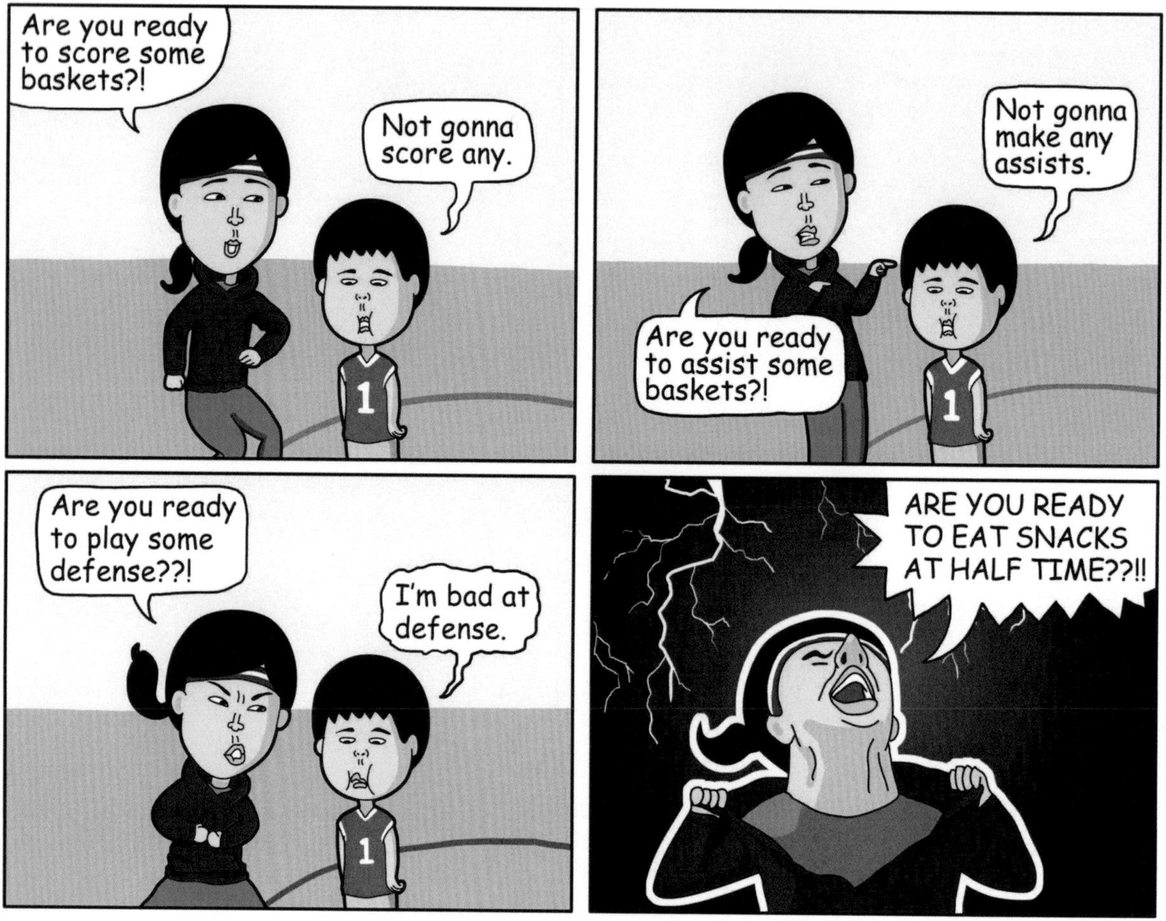
Are you ready to score some baskets?!
Not gonna score any.
Are you ready to assist some baskets?!
Not gonna make any assists.
Are you ready to play some defense??!
I'm bad at defense.
ARE YOU READY TO EAT SNACKS AT HALF TIME??!!

We lost the game.
Well at least you got a good workout.
These are mostly tears.

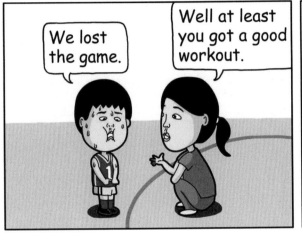

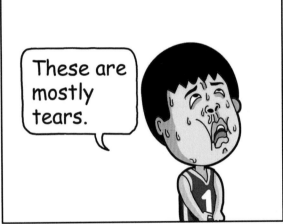

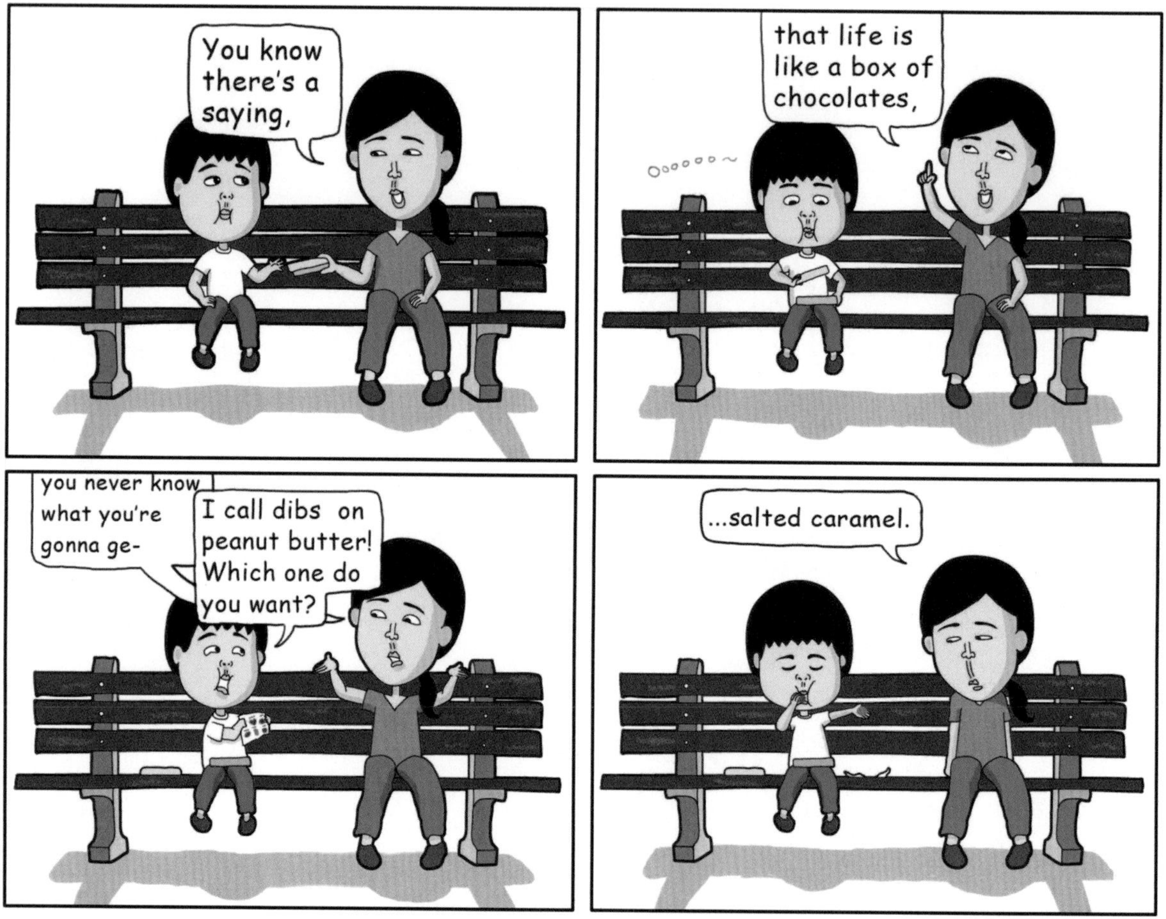
You know there's a saying,
that life is like a box of chocolates,
Oooooo~
you never know what you're gonna ge-
I call dibs on peanut butter! Which one do you want?
...salted caramel.

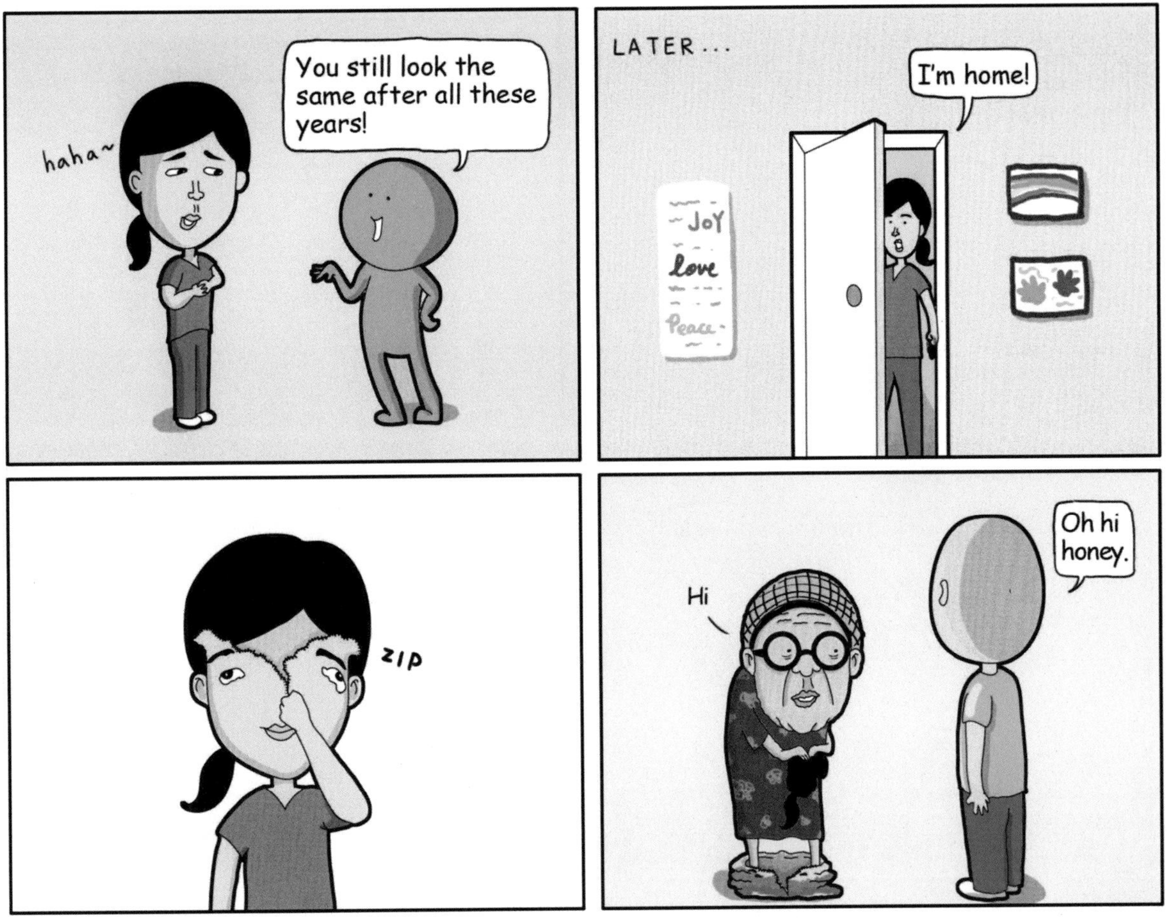
haha~
You still look the same after all these years!
LATER...
I'm home!
JoY
love
Peace
ZIP
Hi
Oh hi honey.

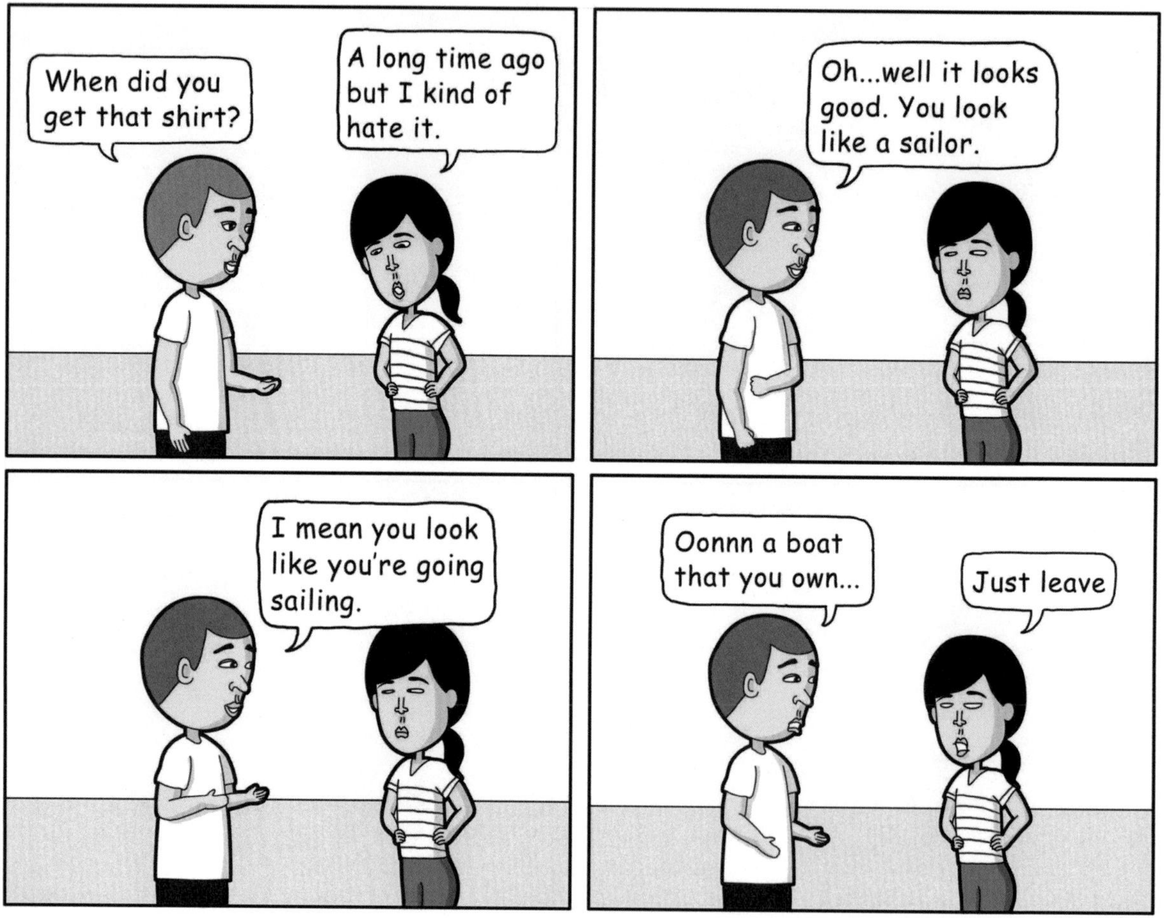
When did you get that shirt?
A long time ago but I kind of hate it.
Oh...well it looks good. You look like a sailor.
I mean you look like you're going sailing.
Oonnn a boat that you own...
Just leave

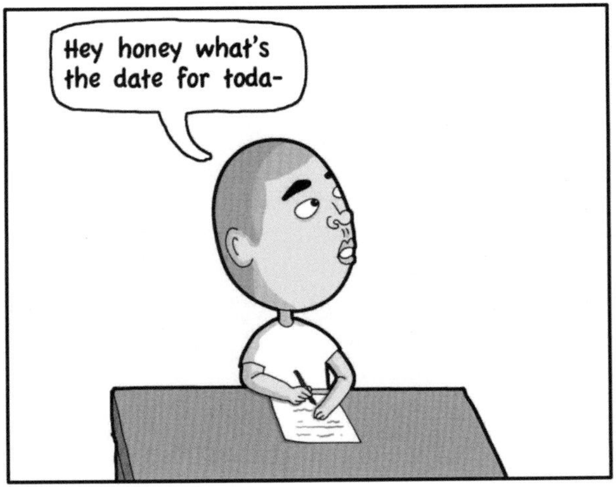
Hey honey what's the date for toda-

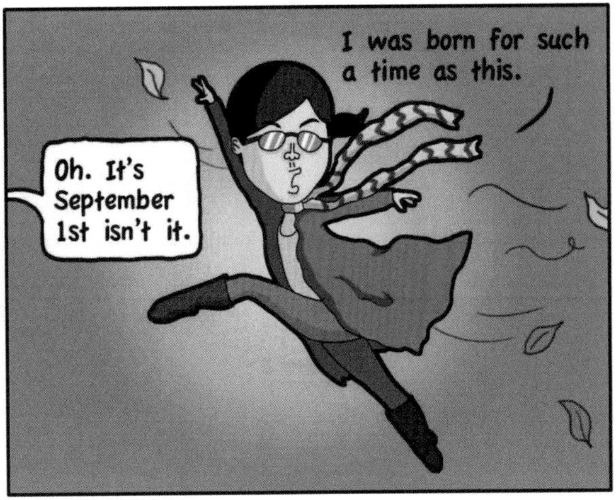
I was born for such a time as this.
Oh. It's September 1st isn't it.

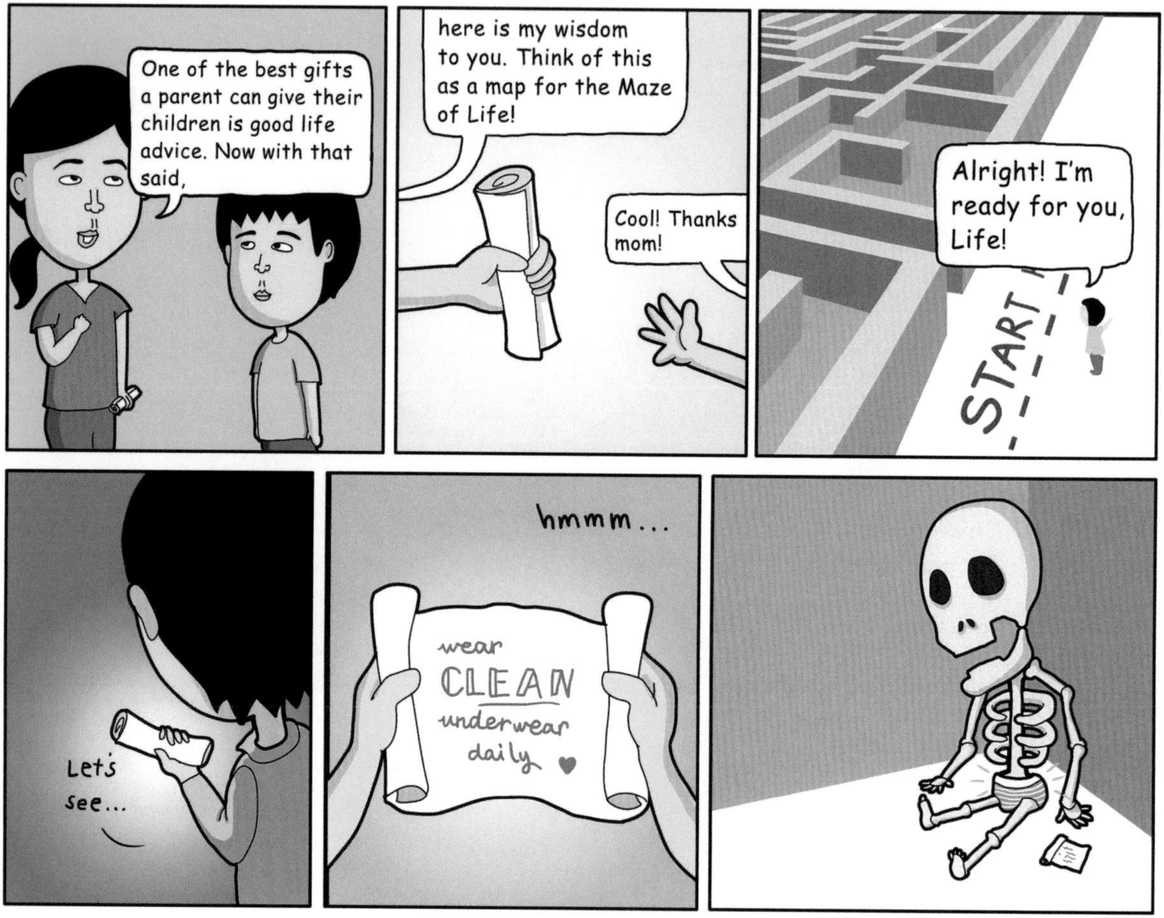
One of the best gifts a parent can give their children is good life advice. Now with that said,
here is my wisdom to you. Think of this as a map for the Maze of Life!
Cool! Thanks mom!
Alright! I'm ready for you, Life!
START
Let's see...
hmmm...
wear CLEAN underwear daily

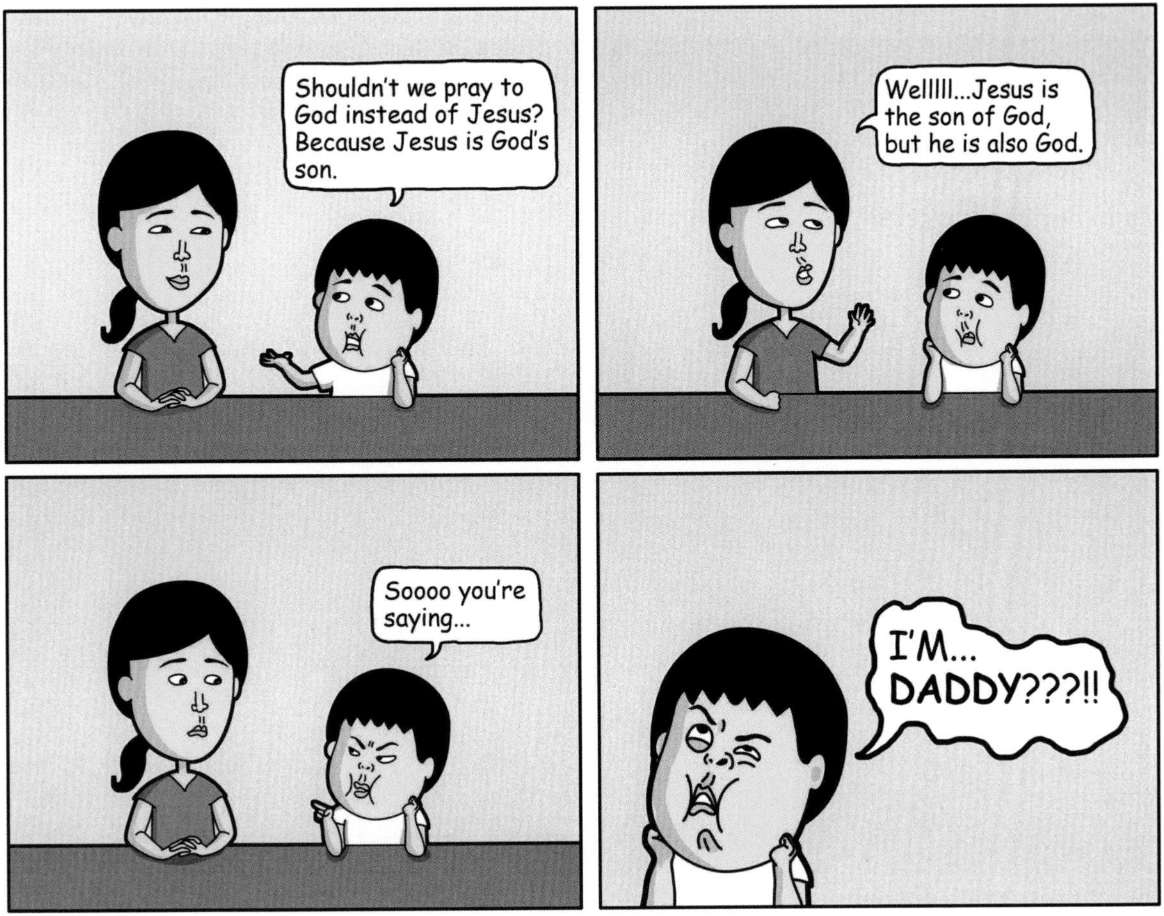
Shouldn't we pray to God instead of Jesus? Because Jesus is God's son.
Welllll...Jesus is the son of God, but he is also God.
Soooo you're saying...
I'M... DADDY???!!

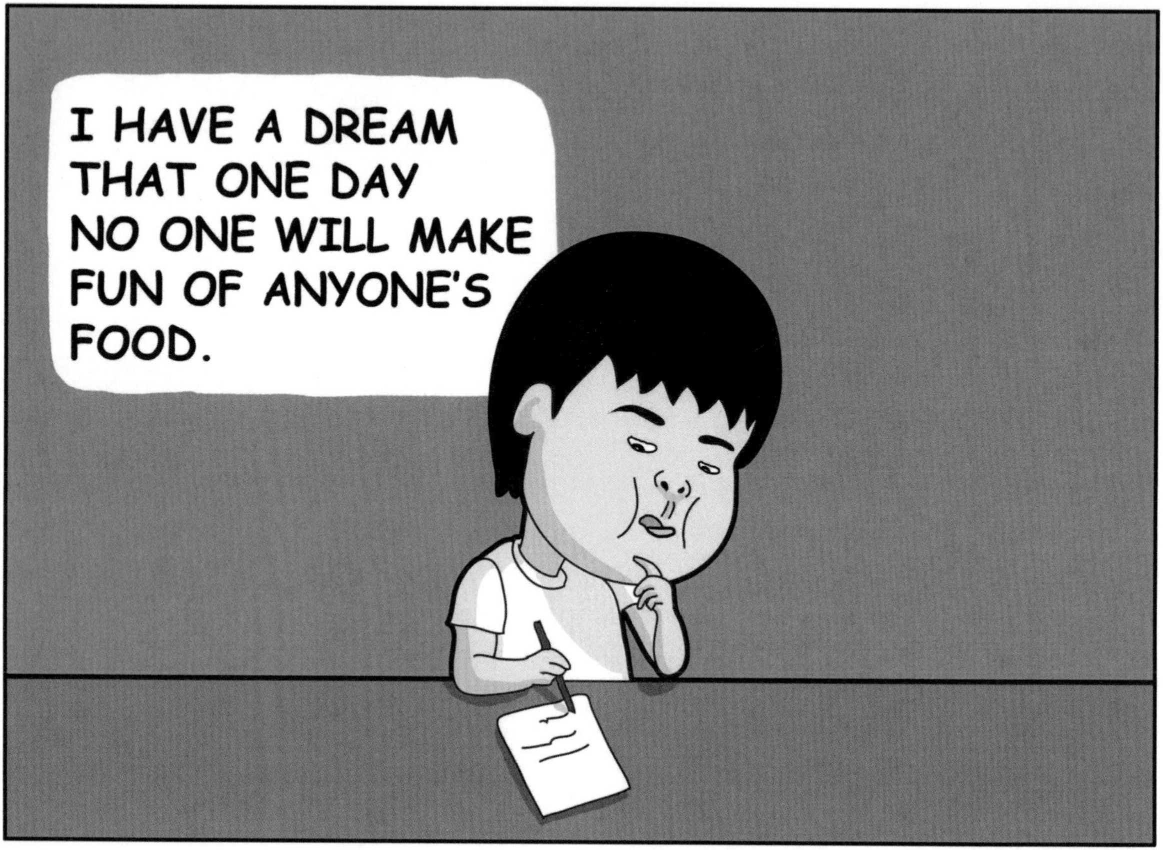
I HAVE A DREAM THAT ONE DAY NO ONE WILL MAKE FUN OF ANYONE'S FOOD.

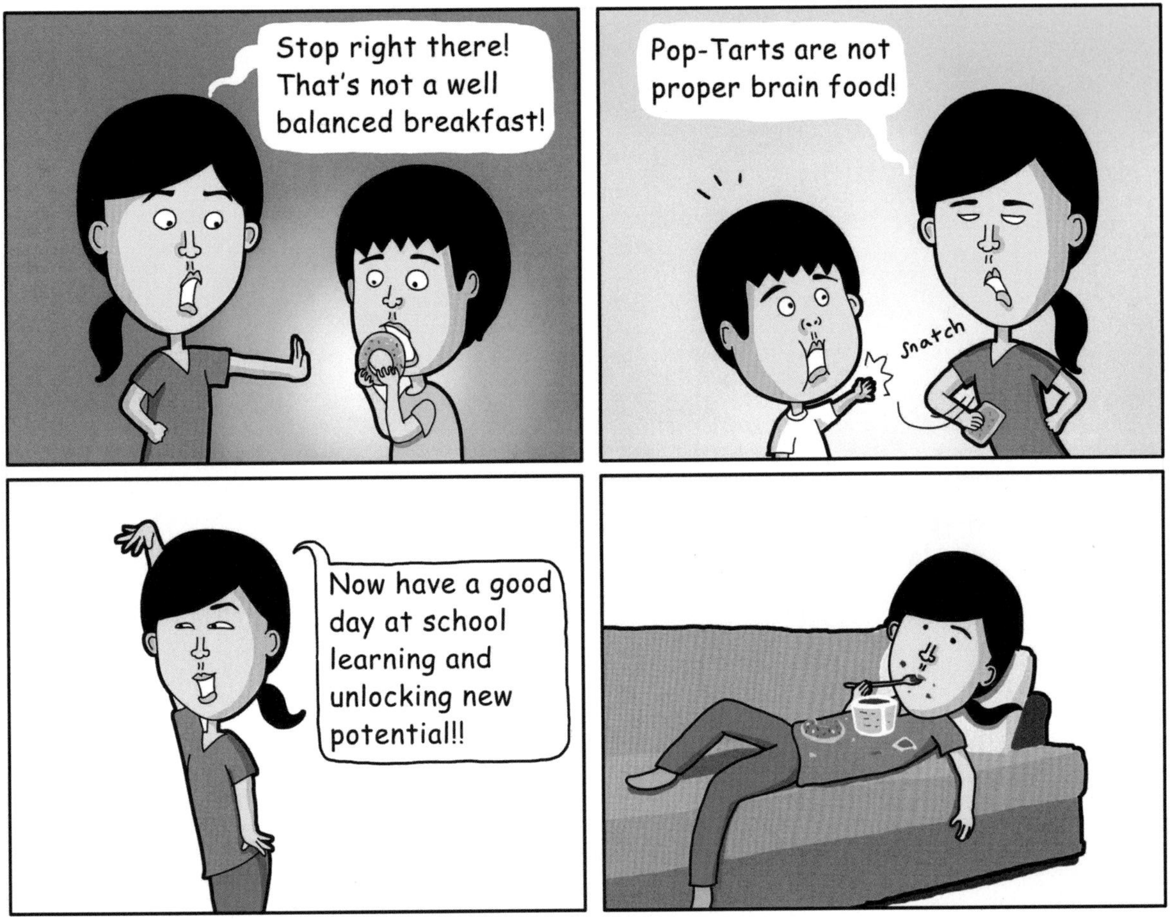
Stop right there! That's not a well balanced breakfast!
Pop-Tarts are not proper brain food!
Snatch
Now have a good day at school learning and unlocking new potential!!

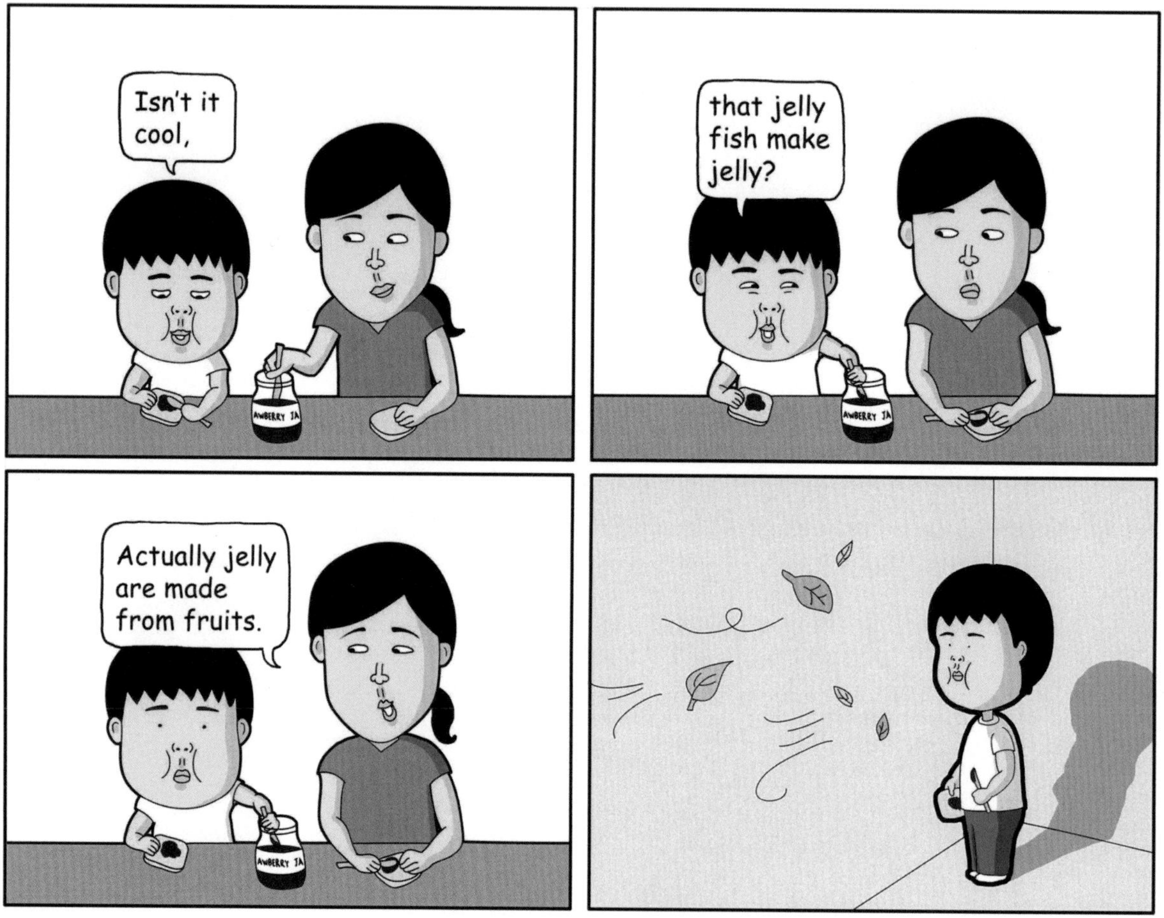
Isn't it cool,
that jelly fish make jelly?
Actually jelly are made from fruits.

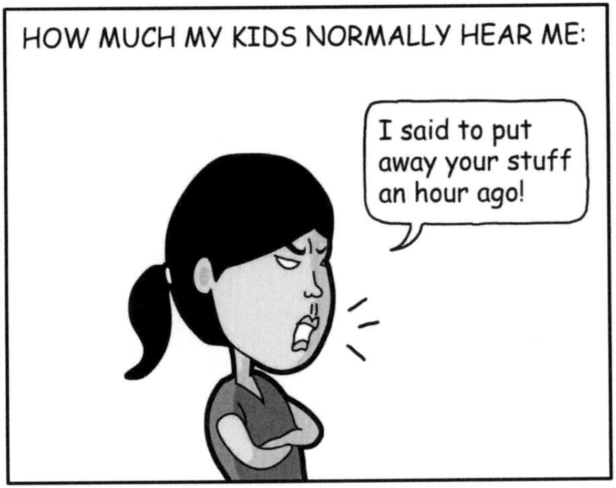
HOW MUCH MY KIDS NORMALLY HEAR ME:
I said to put away your stuff an hour ago!

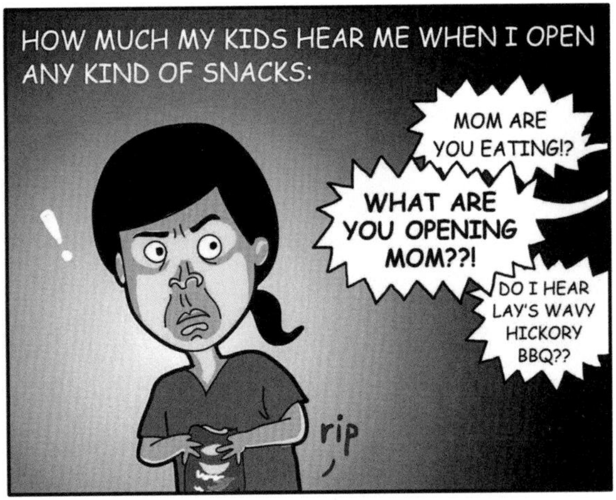
HOW MUCH MY KIDS HEAR ME WHEN I OPEN ANY KIND OF SNACKS:
MOM ARE YOU EATING!?
WHAT ARE YOU OPENING MOM??!
DO I HEAR LAY'S WAVY HICKORY BBQ??
!
rip

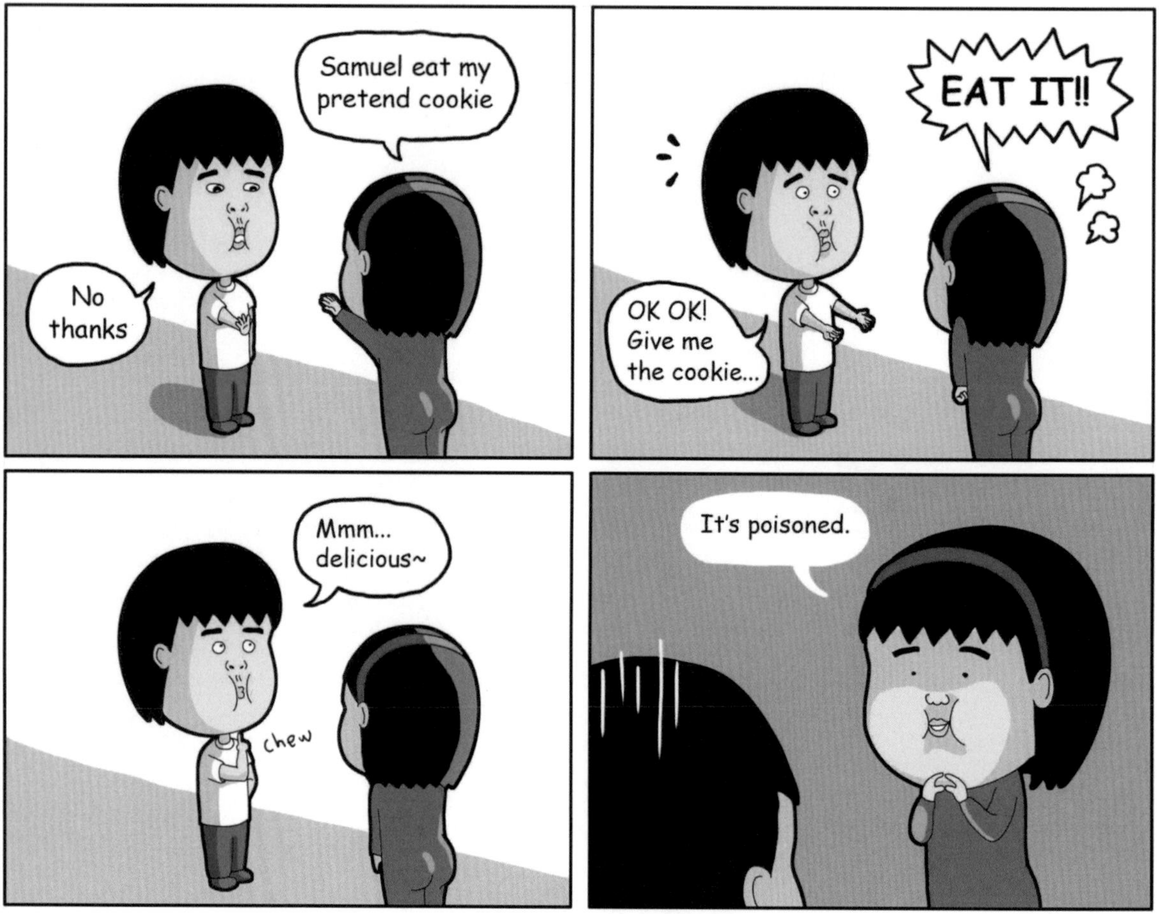
Samuel eat my pretend cookie
No thanks
EAT IT!!
OK OK! Give me the cookie...
Mmm... delicious~
chew
It's poisoned.

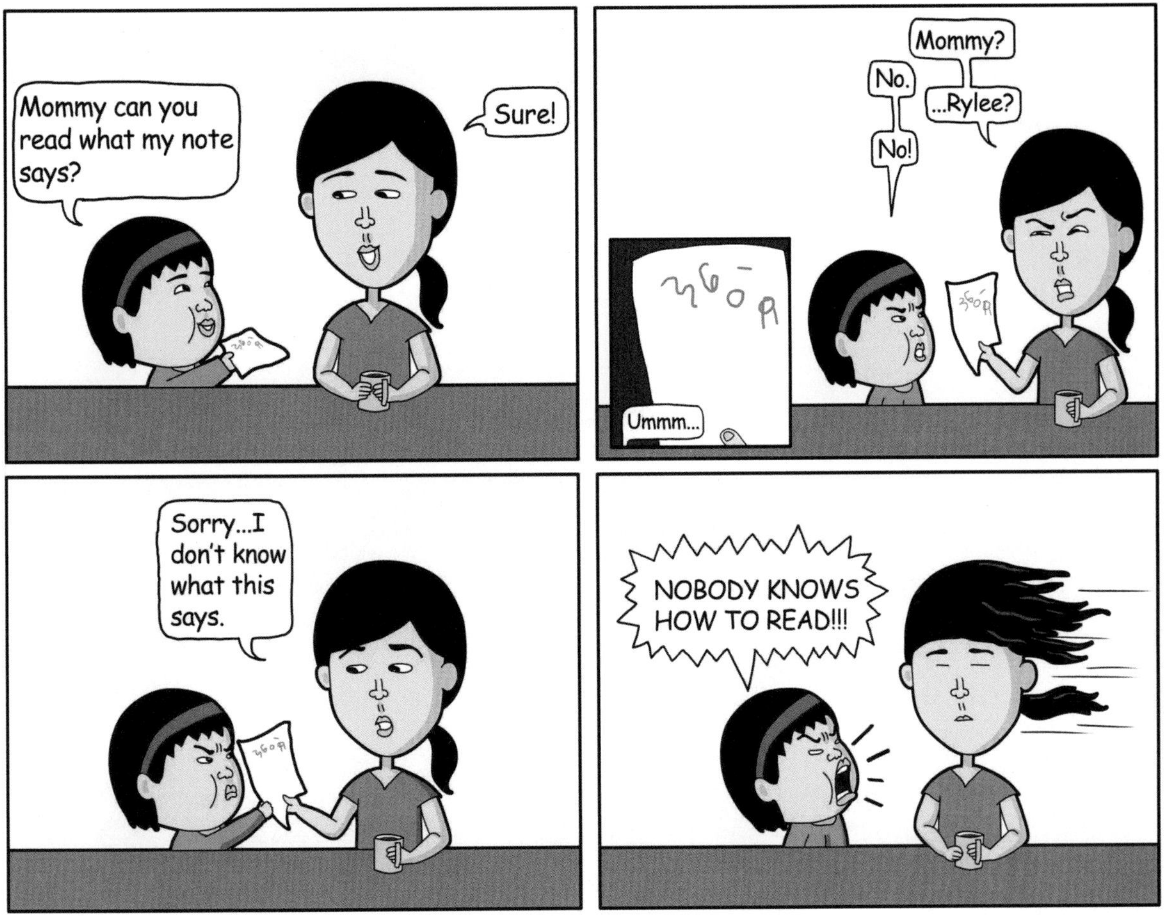
Mommy can you read what my note says?
Sure!
Mommy?
No.
...Rylee?
No!
Ummm...
Sorry...I don't know what this says.
NOBODY KNOWS HOW TO READ!!!

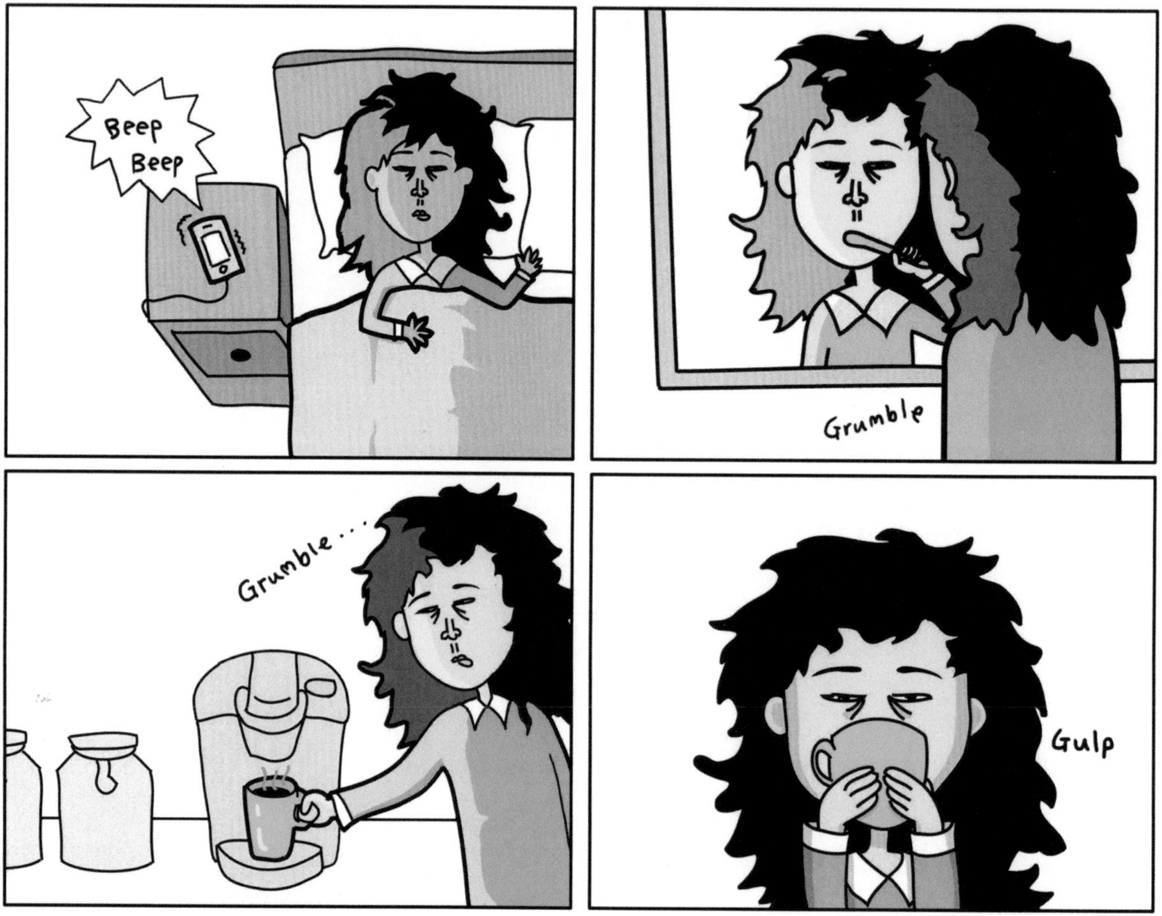
Beep
Beep
Grumble
Grumble....
Gulp

Inhale...

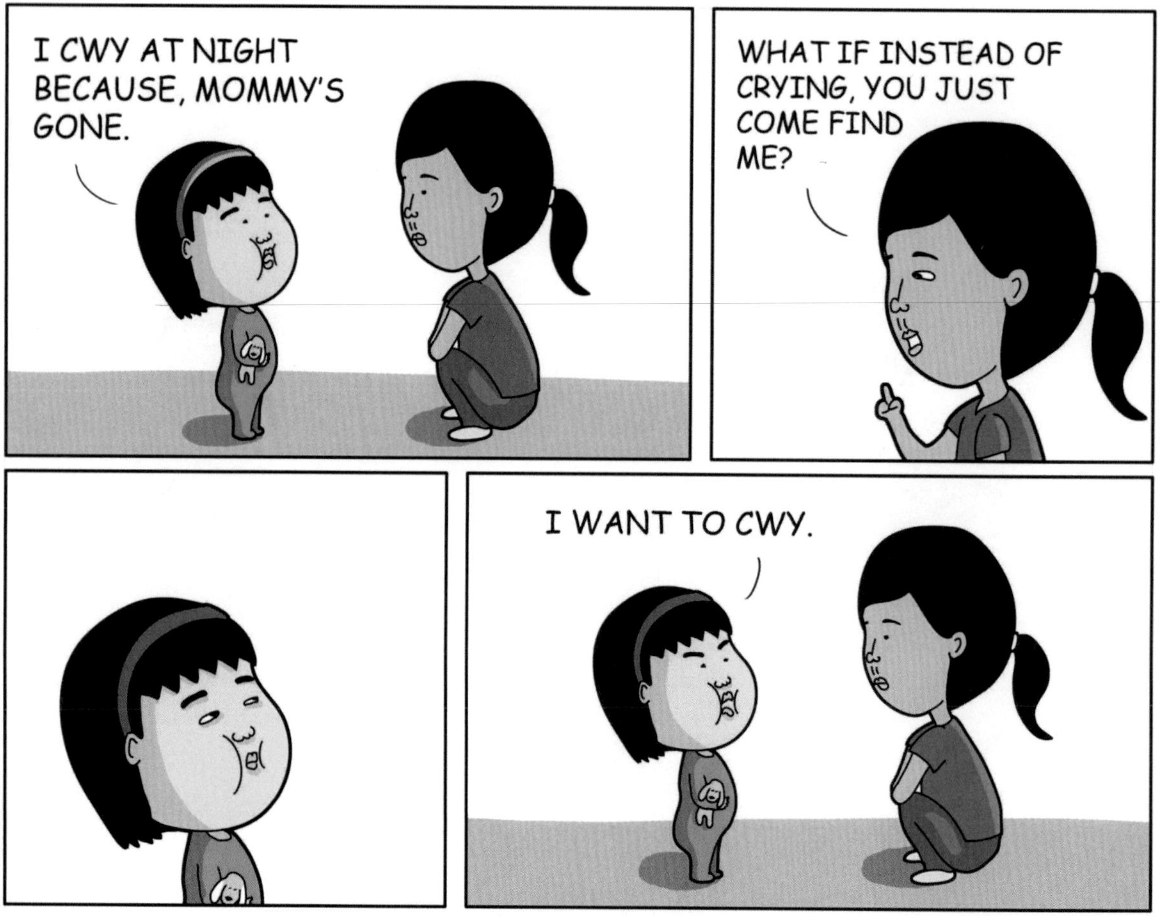
I CWY AT NIGHT BECAUSE, MOMMY'S GONE.
WHAT IF INSTEAD OF CRYING, YOU JUST COME FIND ME?
I WANT TO CWY.

Mom.
Mom I can't breathe.
Pffffttt...

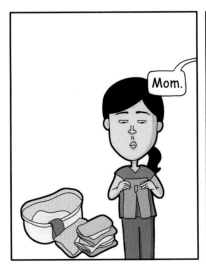

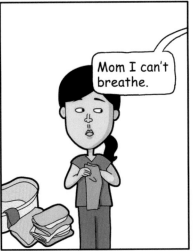

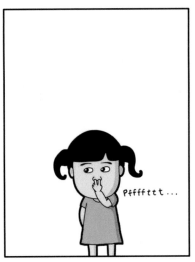

YOU'RE ANNOYING! YOU'RE AN ANNOYING LITTLE BABY!
NO I'M NOT!! I'M RYLEE!!!!

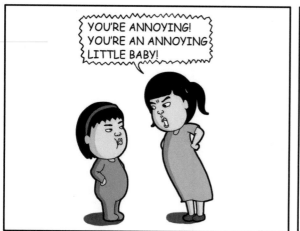

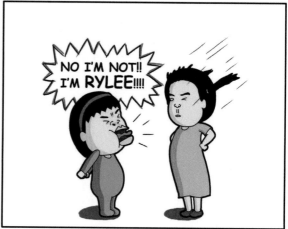

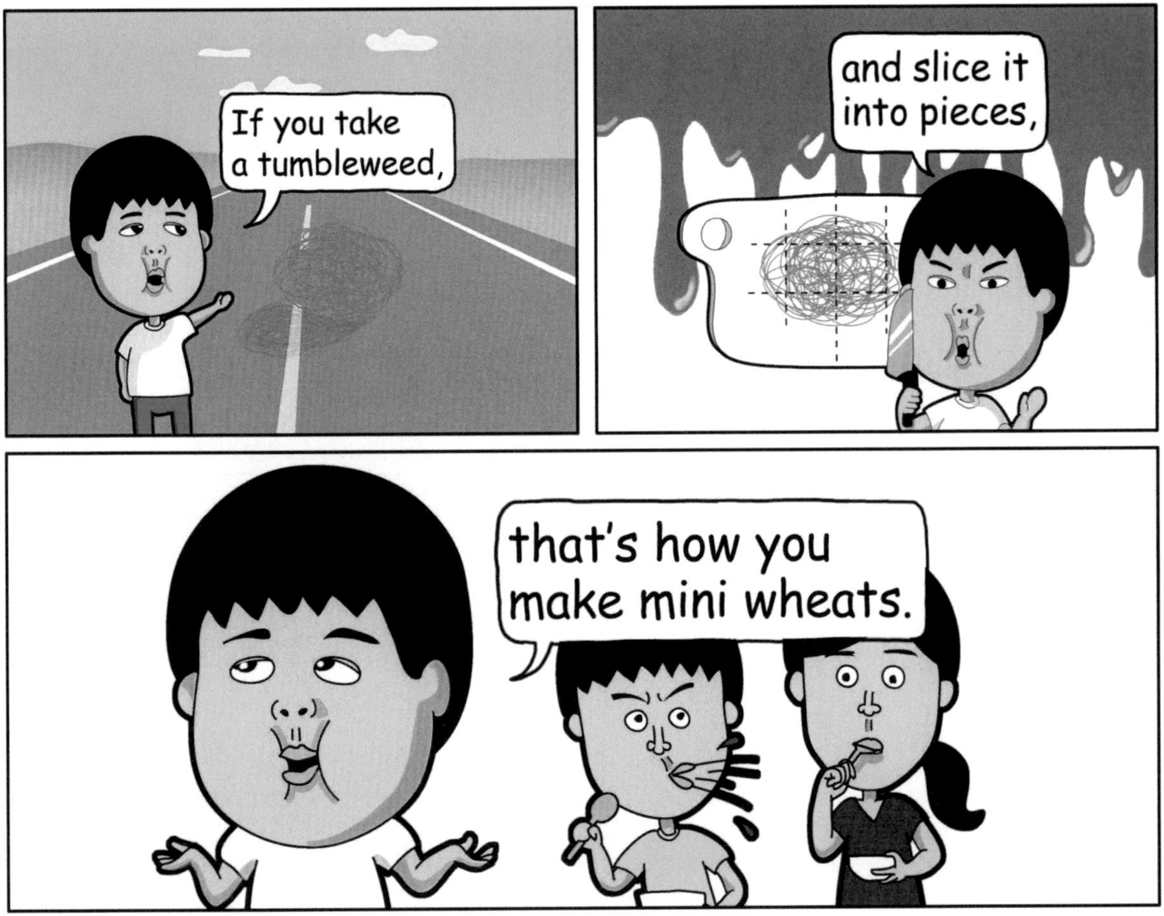
If you take a tumbleweed,
and slice it into pieces,
that's how you make mini wheats.

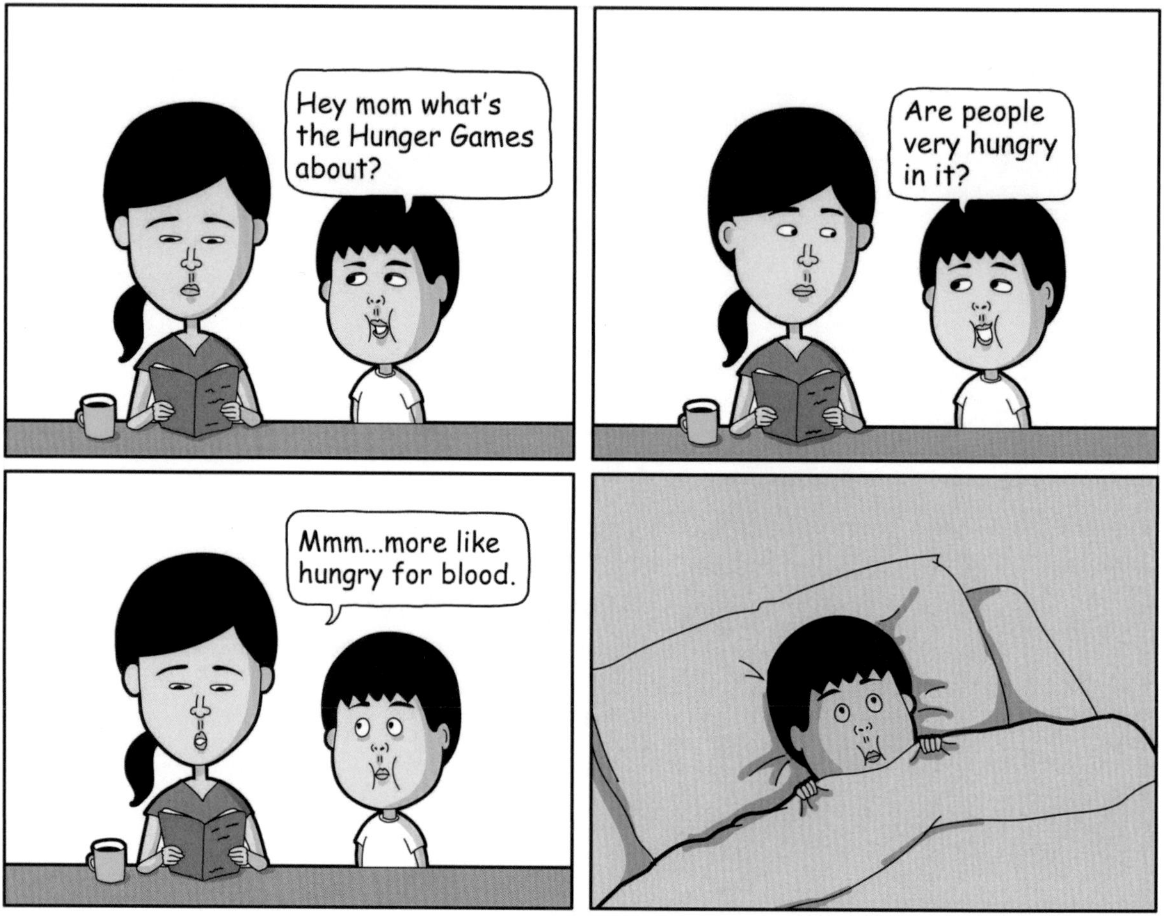
Hey mom what's the Hunger Games about?
Are people very hungry in it?
Mmm...more like hungry for blood.

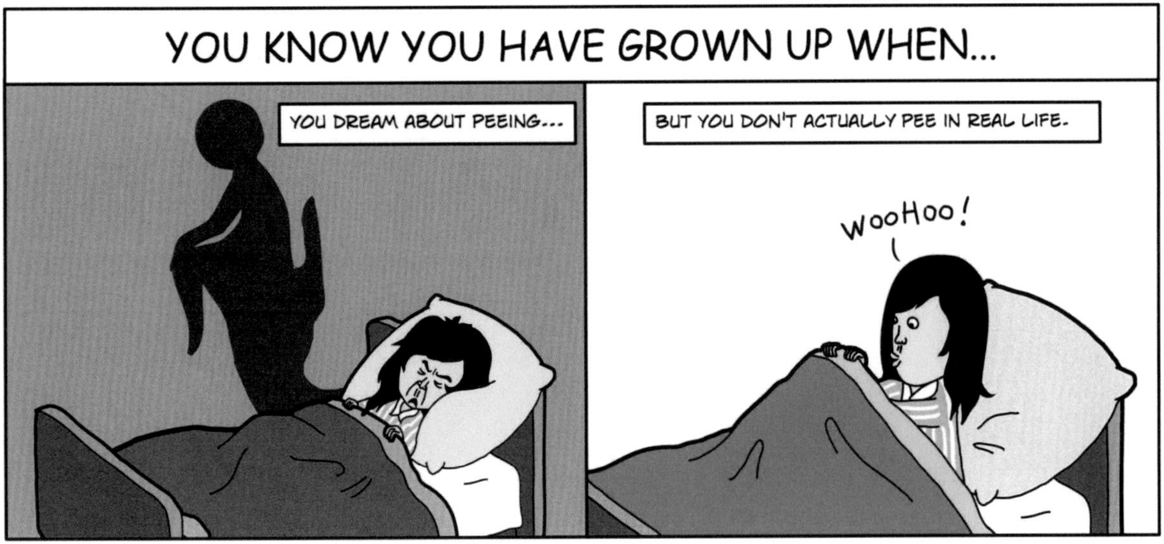
YOU KNOW YOU HAVE GROWN UP WHEN...
YOU DREAM ABOUT PEEING...
BUT YOU DON'T ACTUALLY PEE IN REAL LIFE.
WooHoo!

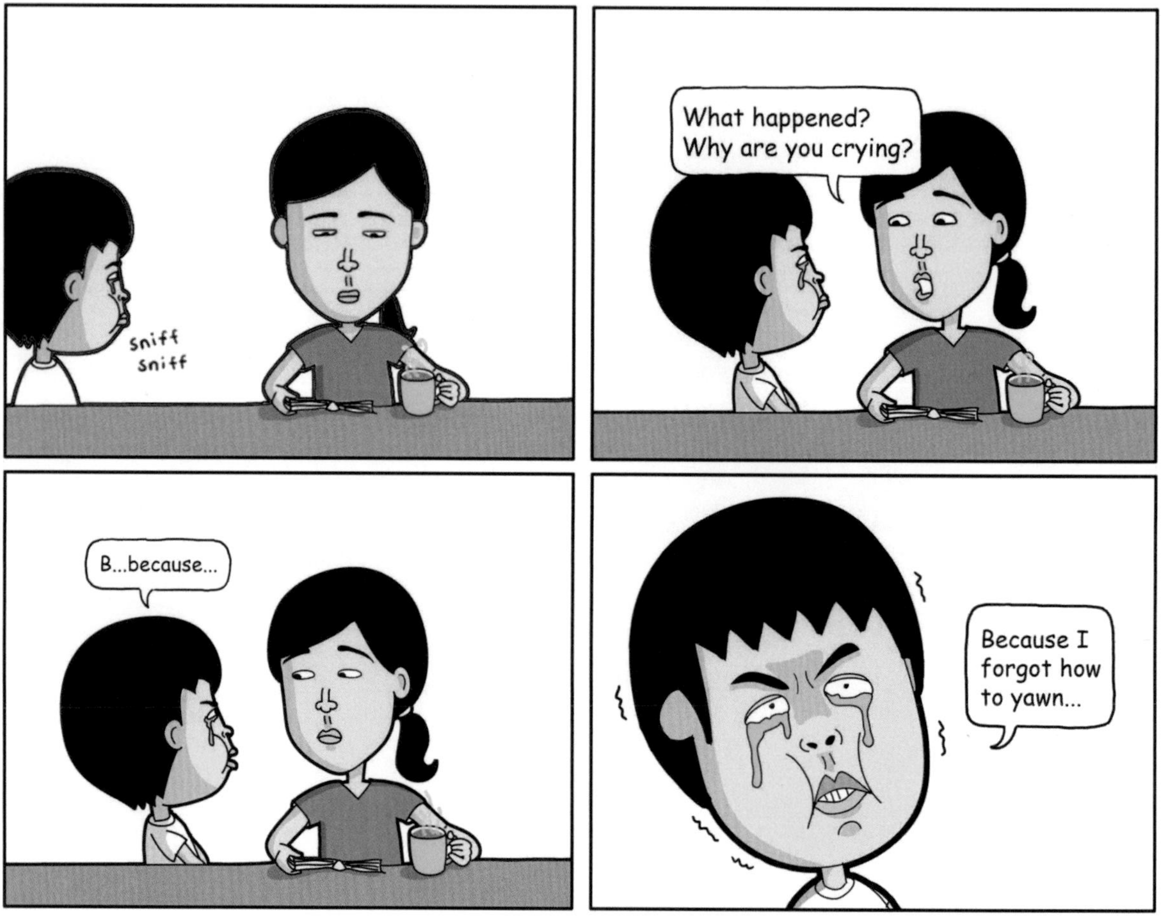
sniff
sniff
What happened?
Why are you crying?
B...because...
Because I
forgot how
to yawn...

You guys picked a good country to live in.
Why do you think that?
Because I can understand things people say.

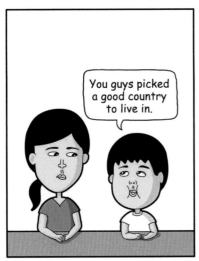

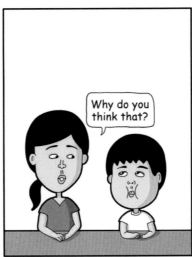

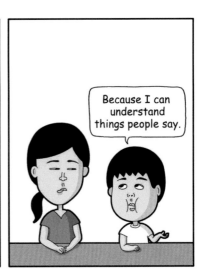

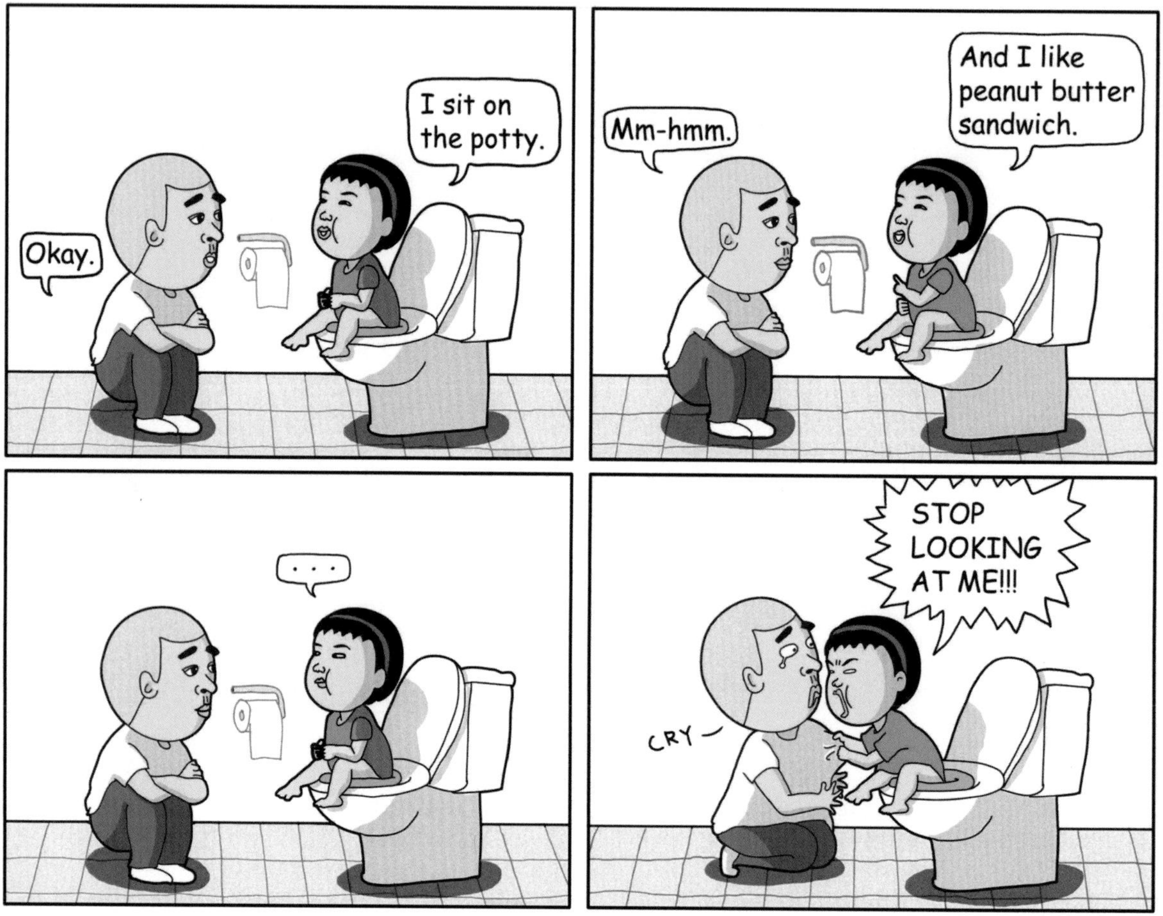
I sit on the potty.
Okay.
And I like peanut butter sandwich.
Mm-hmm.
. . .
STOP LOOKING AT ME!!!
CRY

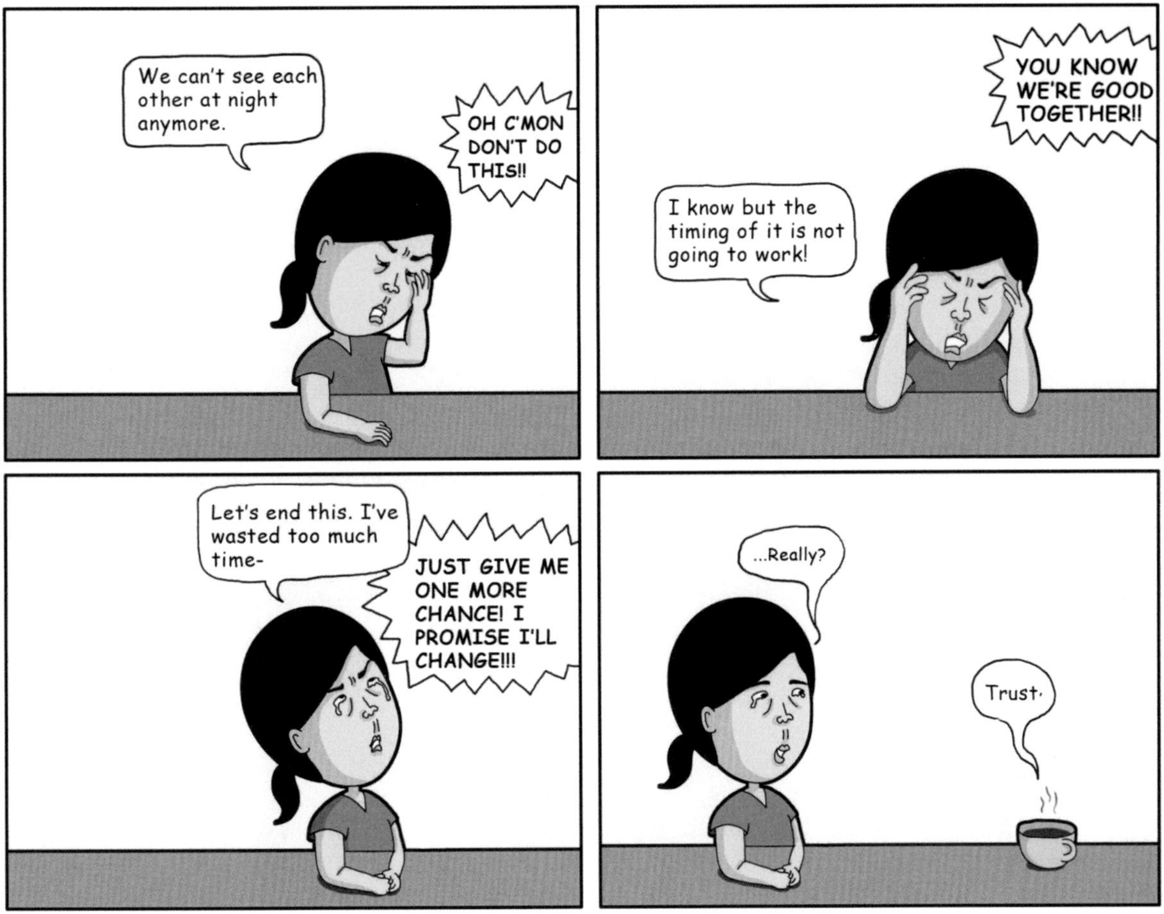
We can't see each other at night anymore.
OH C'MON DON'T DO THIS!!
YOU KNOW WE'RE GOOD TOGETHER!!
I know but the timing of it is not going to work!
Let's end this. I've wasted too much time-
JUST GIVE ME ONE MORE CHANCE! I PROMISE I'LL CHANGE!!!
...Really?
Trust.

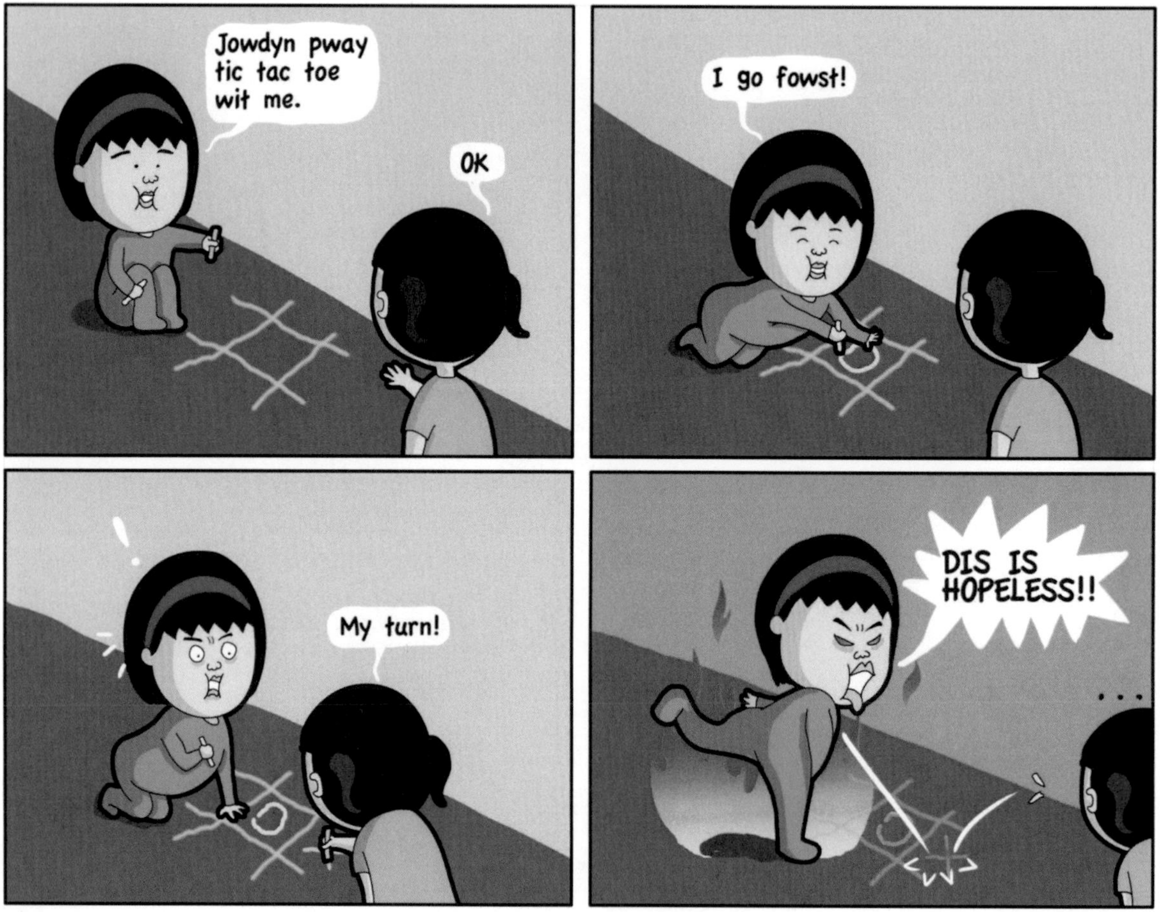
Jowdyn pway tic tac toe wit me.
OK
I go fowst!
!
My turn!
DIS IS HOPELESS!!
...

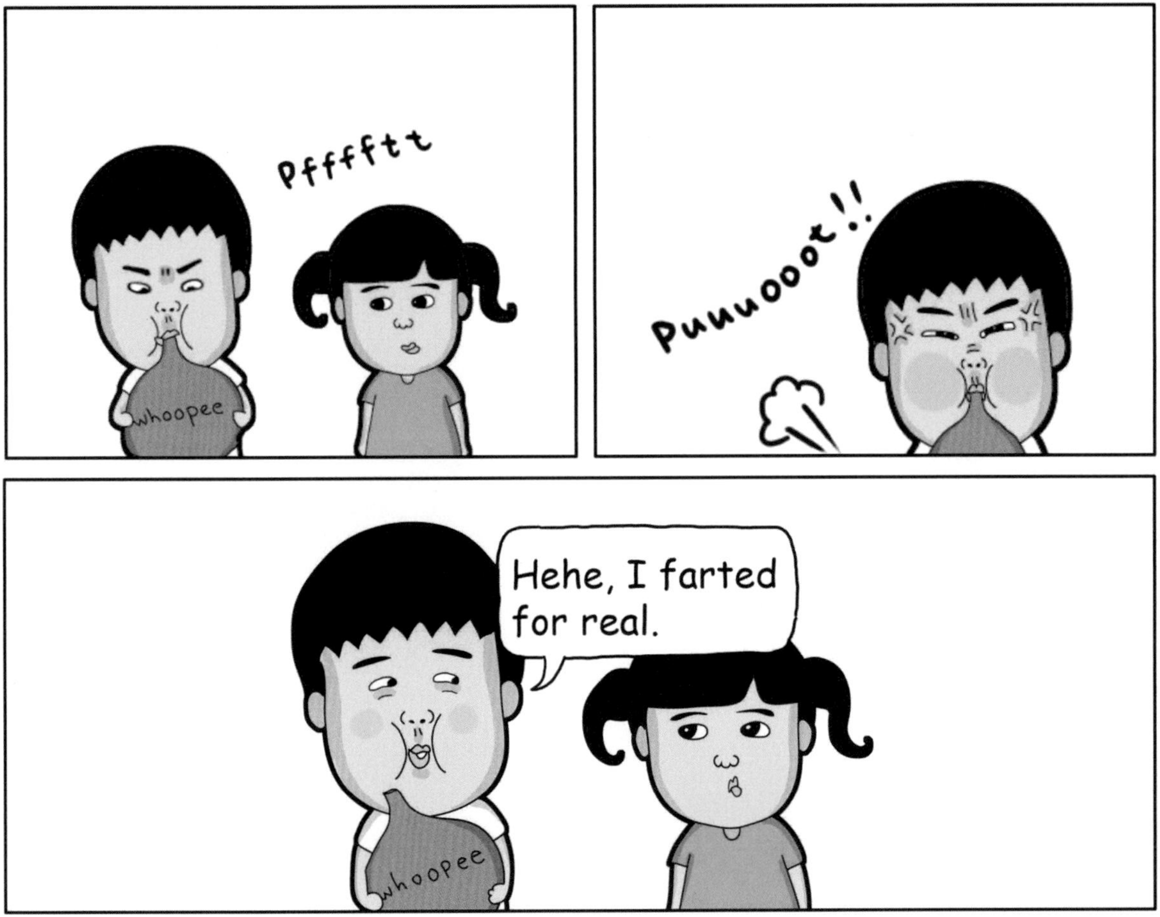
Pfffftt
whoopee
Puuuooot!!
Hehe, I farted for real.
whoopee

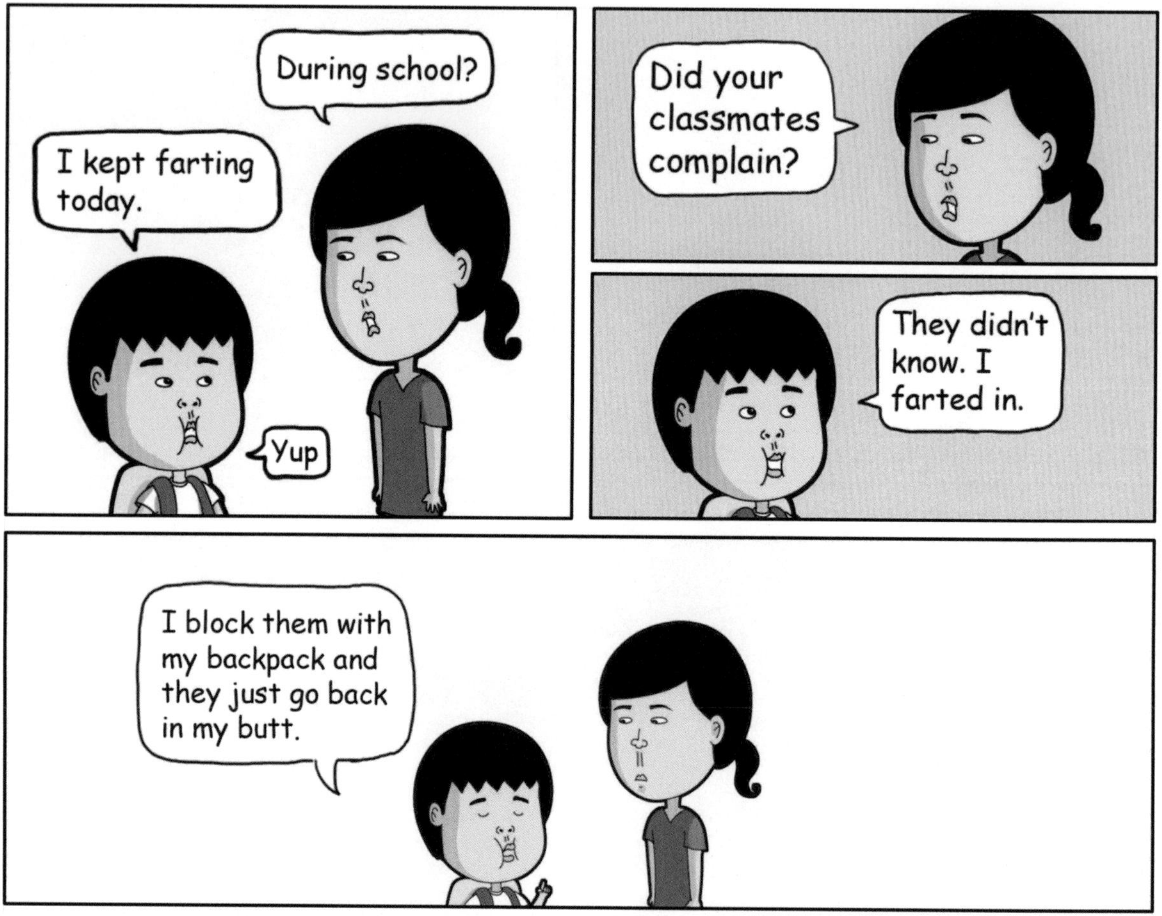
I kept farting today.
During school?
Yup
Did your classmates complain?
They didn't know. I farted in.
I block them with my backpack and they just go back in my butt.

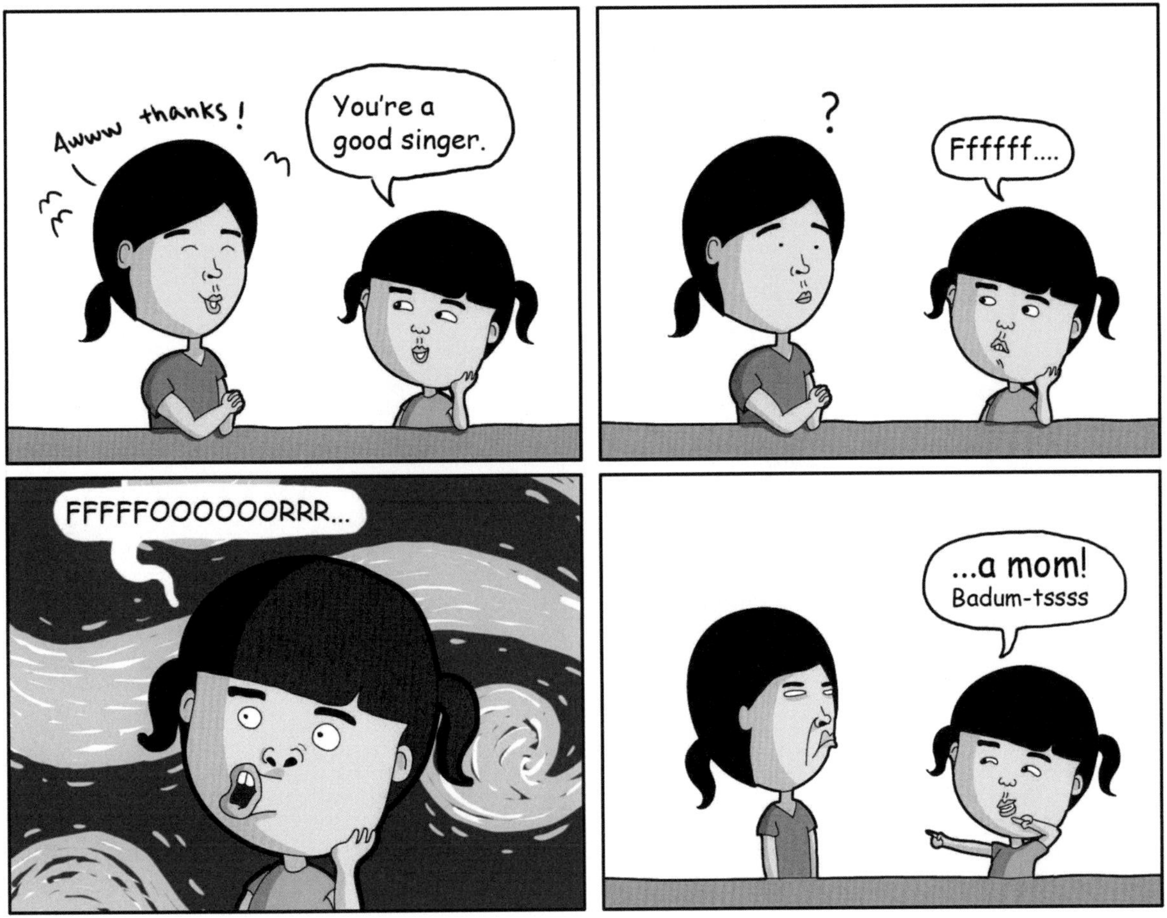
Awww thanks!
You're a good singer.
?
Ffffff....
FFFFFOOOOOORRR...
...a mom!
Badum-tssss

You know how I know that Cinderella is fake?
Because **NOBODY** can stay up until midnight!

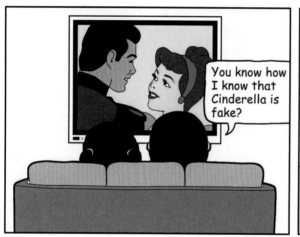

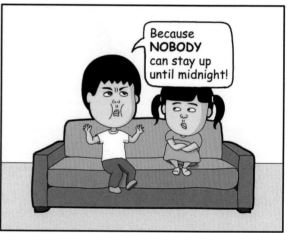

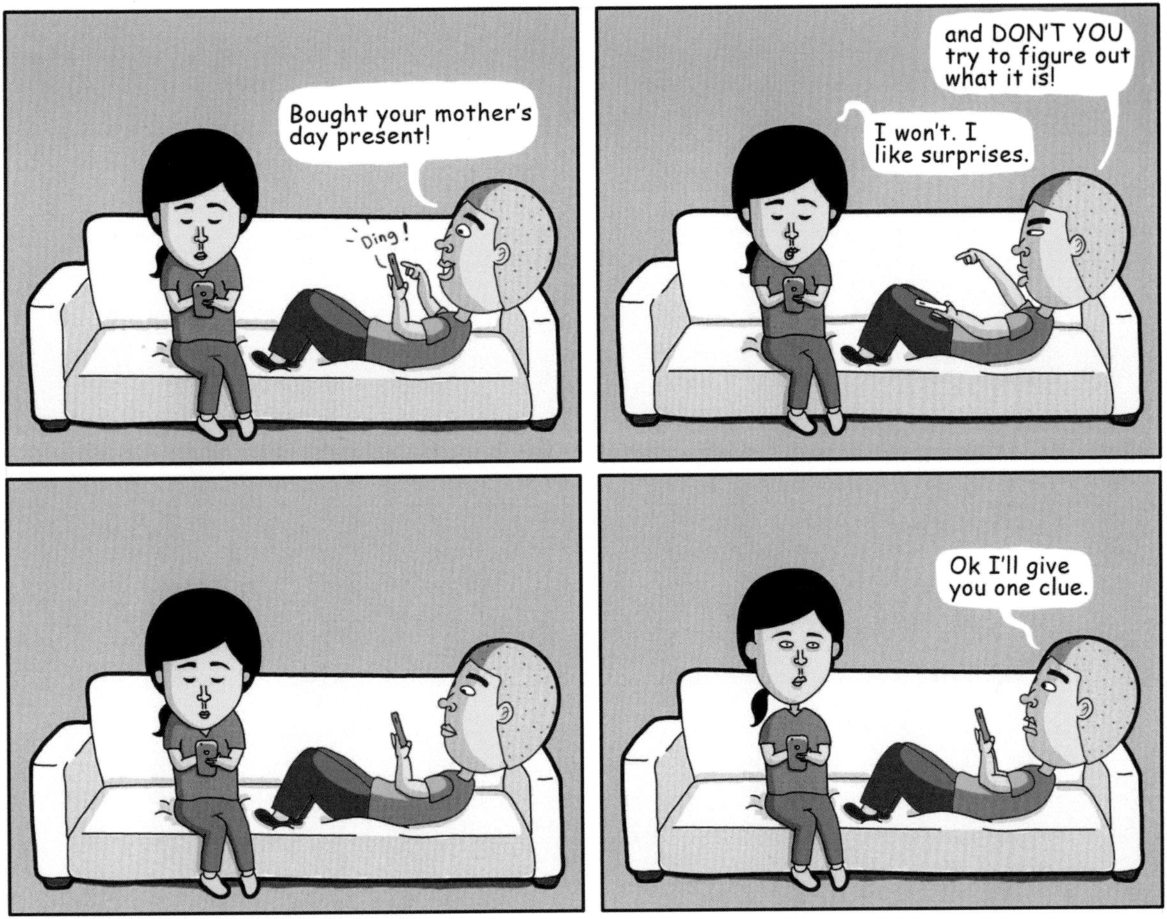
Bought your mother's day present!
Ding!
and DON'T YOU try to figure out what it is!
I won't. I like surprises.
Ok I'll give you one clue.

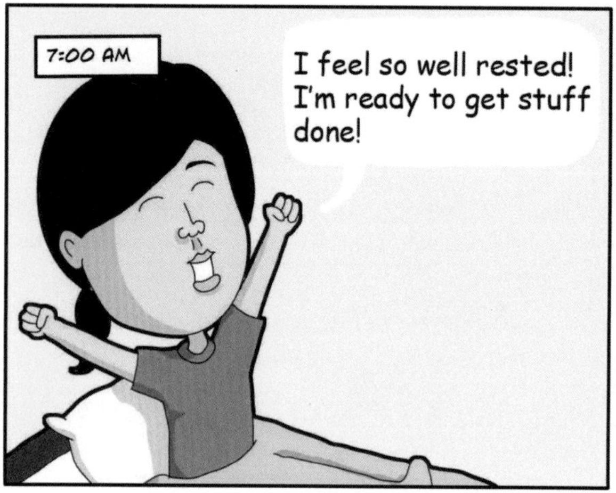
7:00 AM
I feel so well rested! I'm ready to get stuff done!

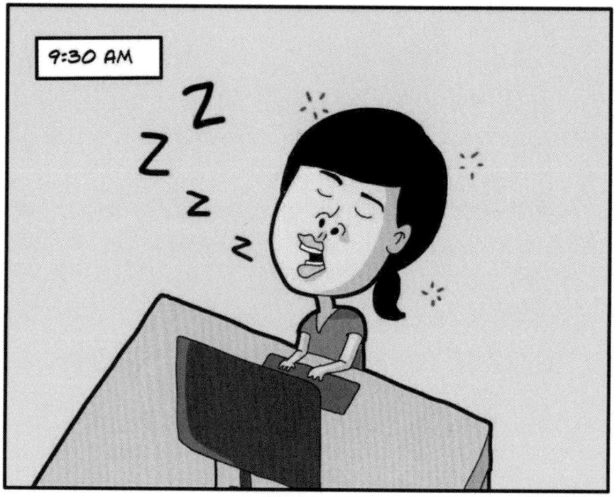
9:30 AM
Z Z z z

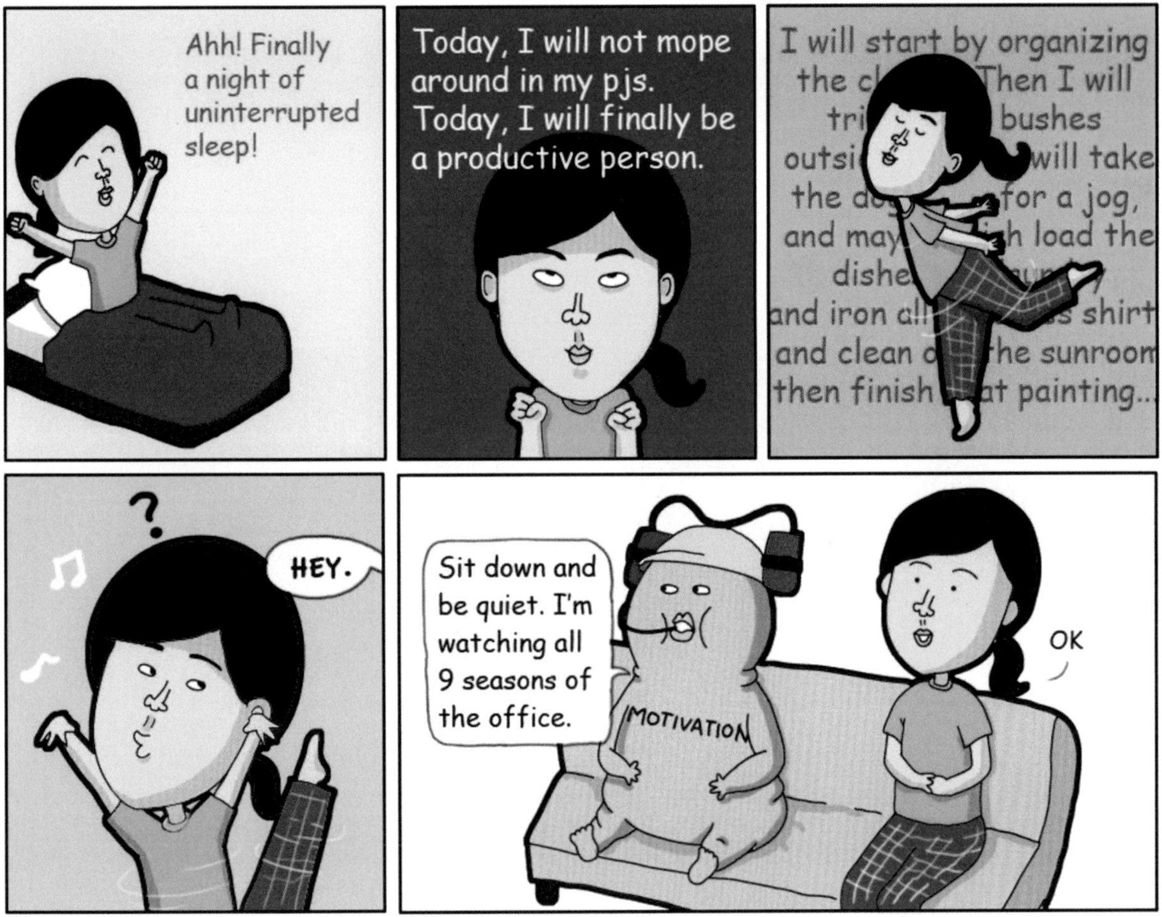
Ahh! Finally a night of uninterrupted sleep!
Today, I will not mope around in my pjs. Today, I will finally be a productive person.
I will start by organizing
the c Then I will
tri bushes
outsi will take
the do for a jog,
and may h load the
dishe
and iron all s shirt
and clean o the sunroom
then finish at painting...
?
HEY.
Sit down and be quiet. I'm watching all 9 seasons of the office.
MOTIVATION
OK

I like your haircut!
Aww thanks! But I didn't get a haircut.
Oh. Well then I like your eyeball.

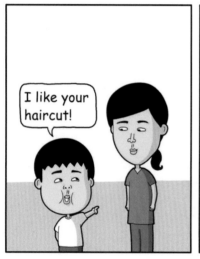

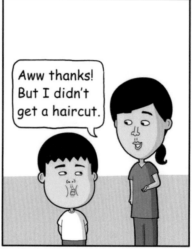

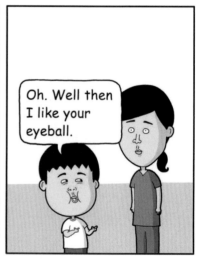

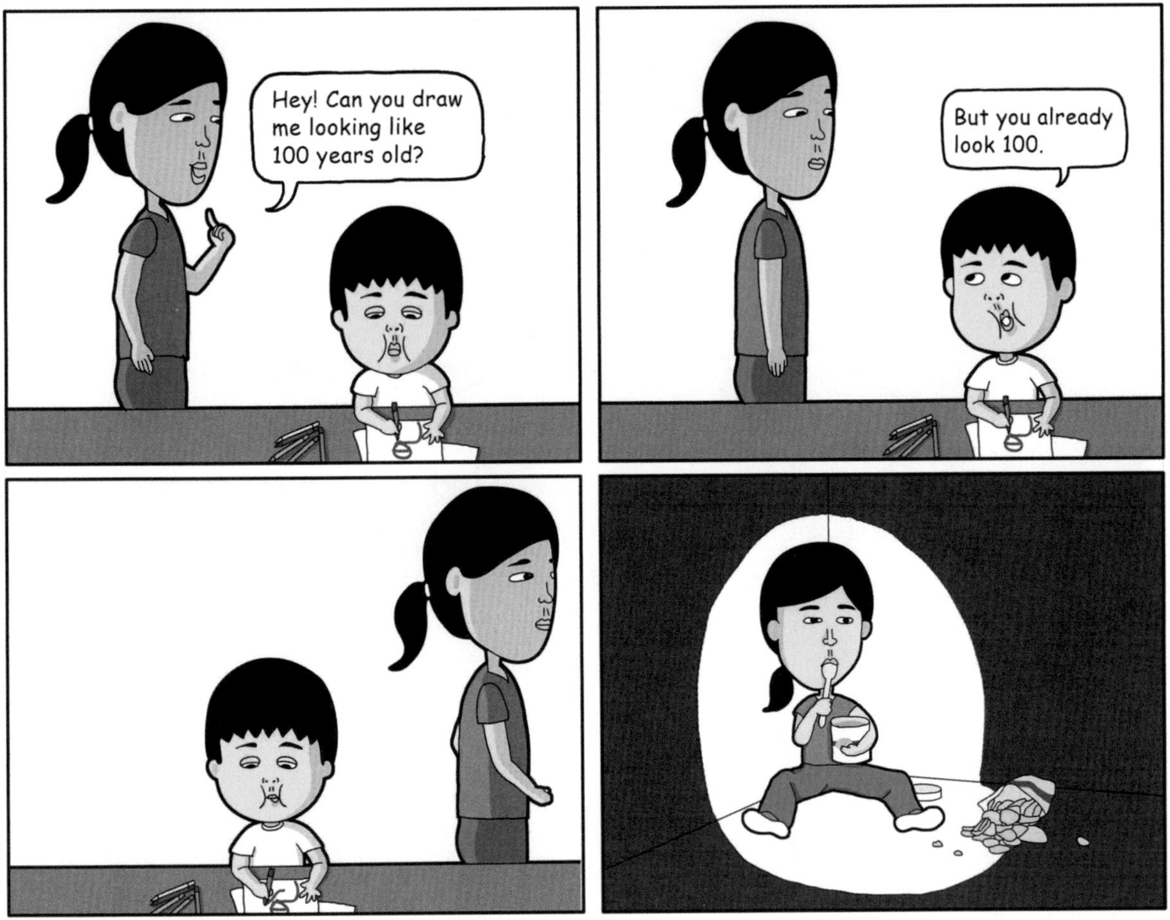
Hey! Can you draw me looking like 100 years old?
But you already look 100.

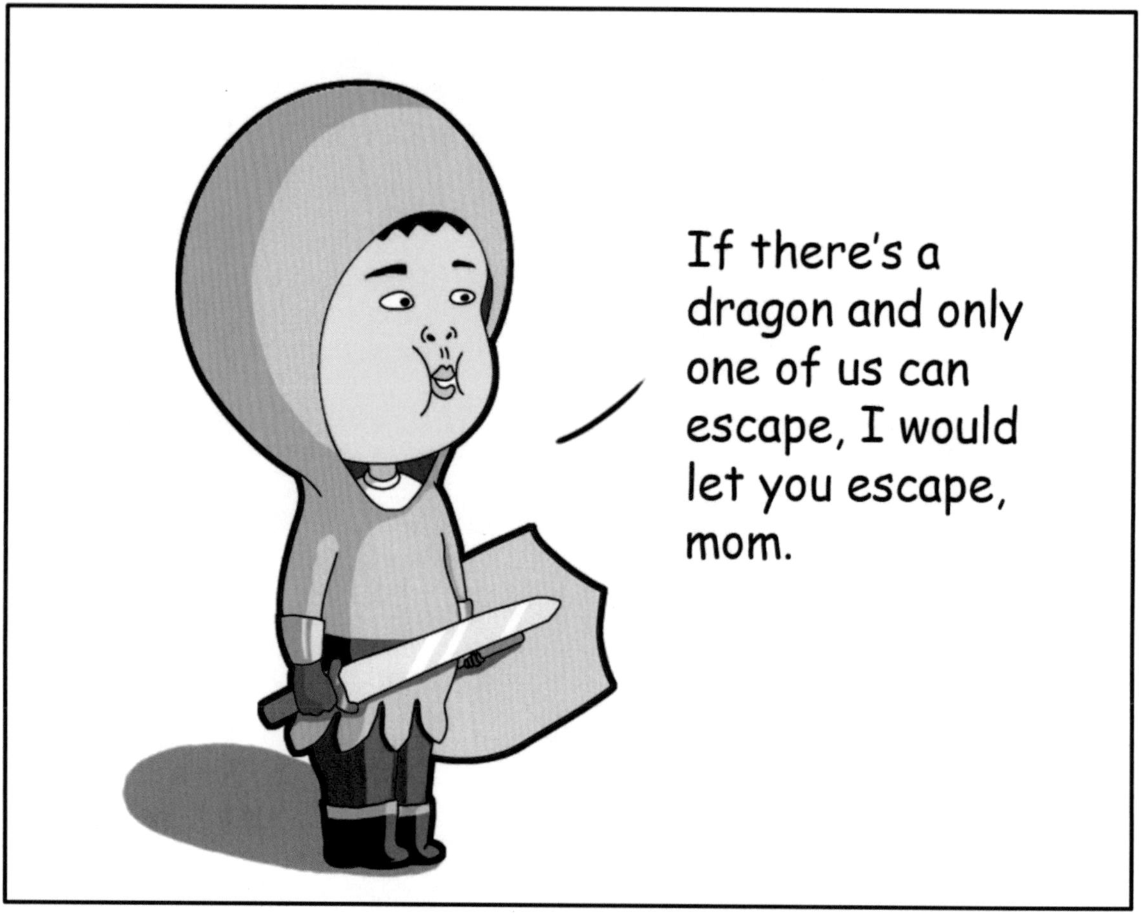
If there's a dragon and only one of us can escape, I would let you escape, mom.

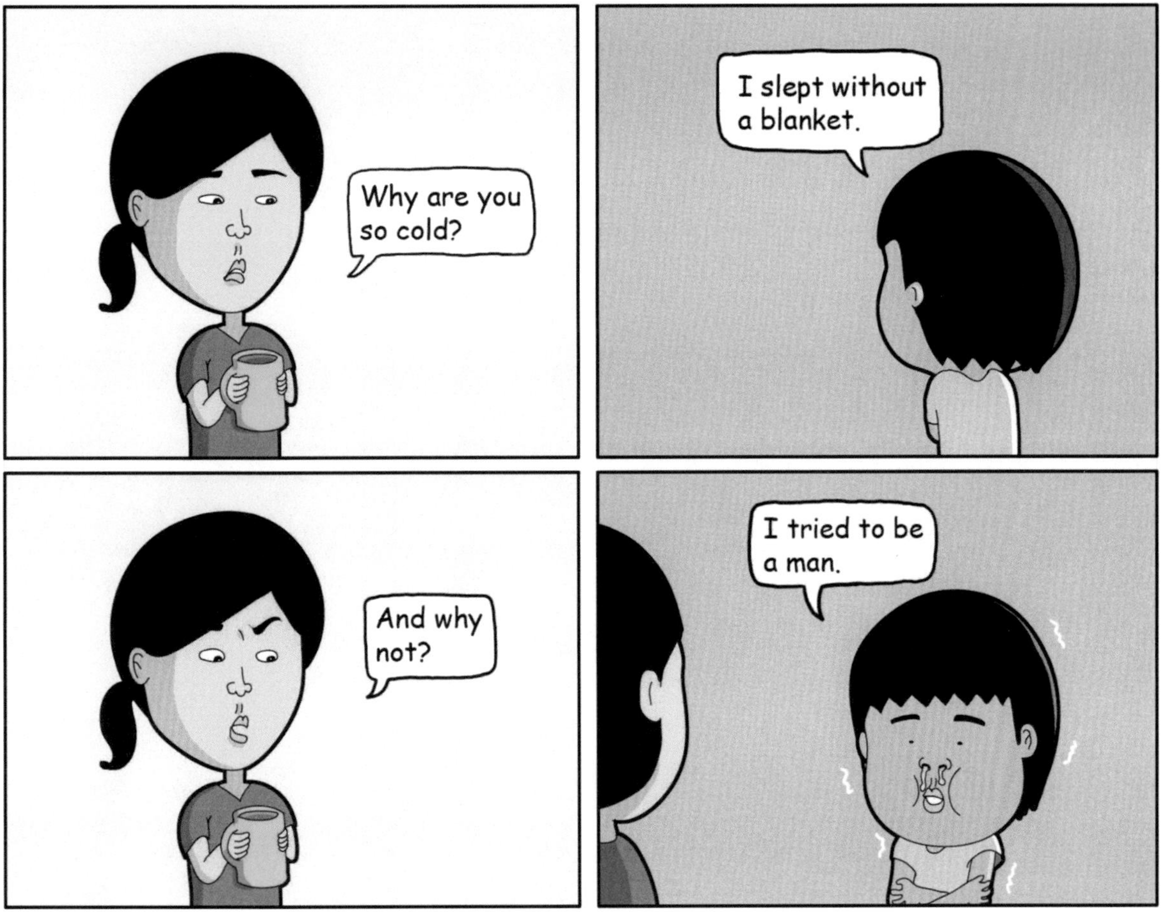
Why are you so cold?
I slept without a blanket.
And why not?
I tried to be a man.

Daddy! Come wipe me!
Woah! Why is your poop green?
Because I eat grass.

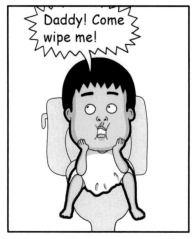

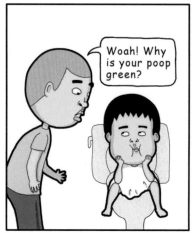

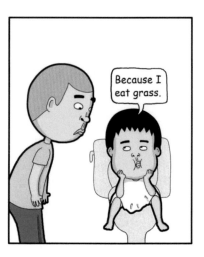

CREEEEEEEEAK
SHUFFLE
SHUFFLE
AAAHHHHHH!!!
SHUFFLE
Can I have breakfast?

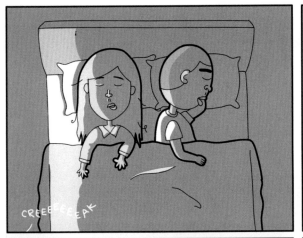

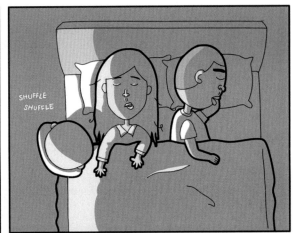

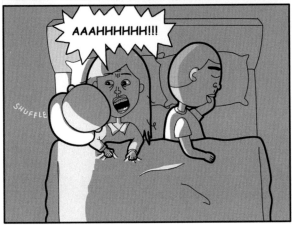

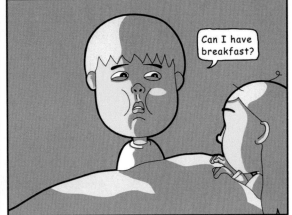

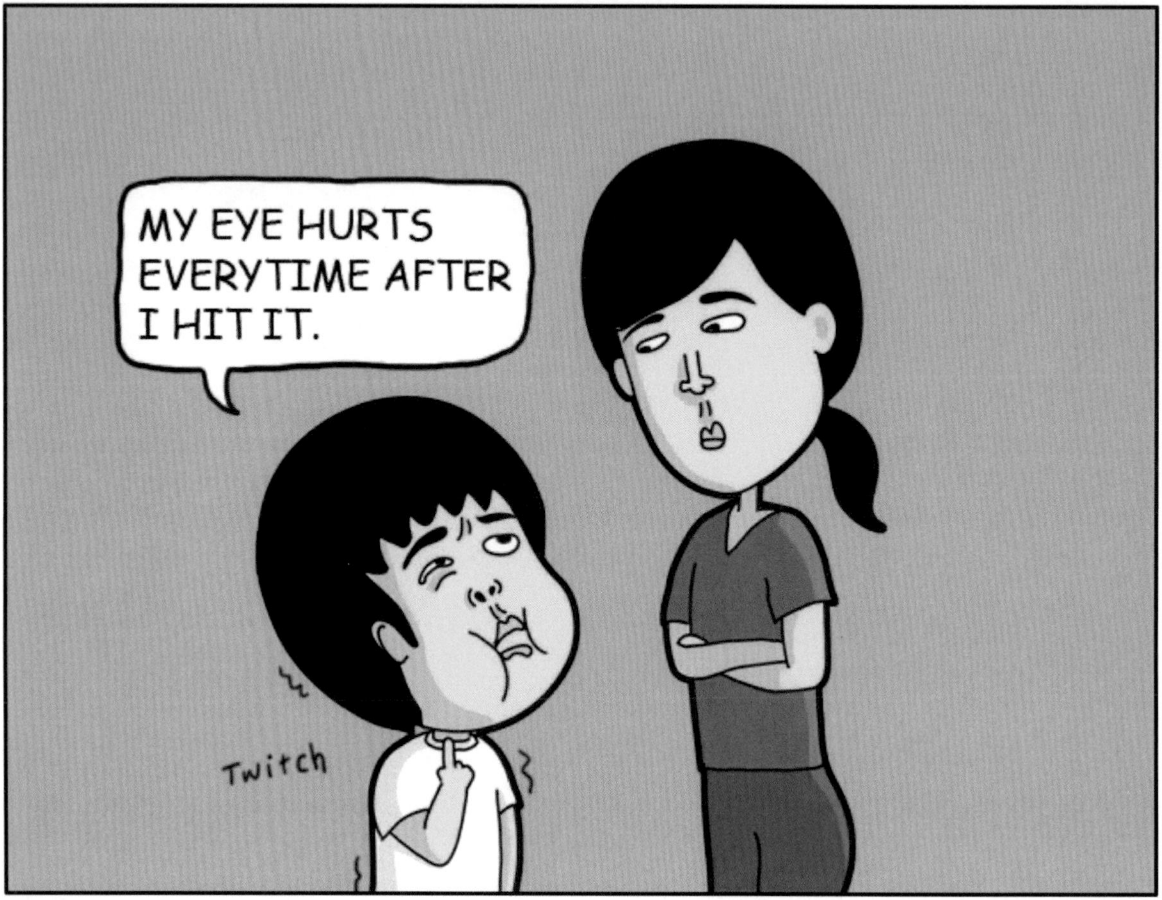
MY EYE HURTS EVERYTIME AFTER I HIT IT.
Twitch

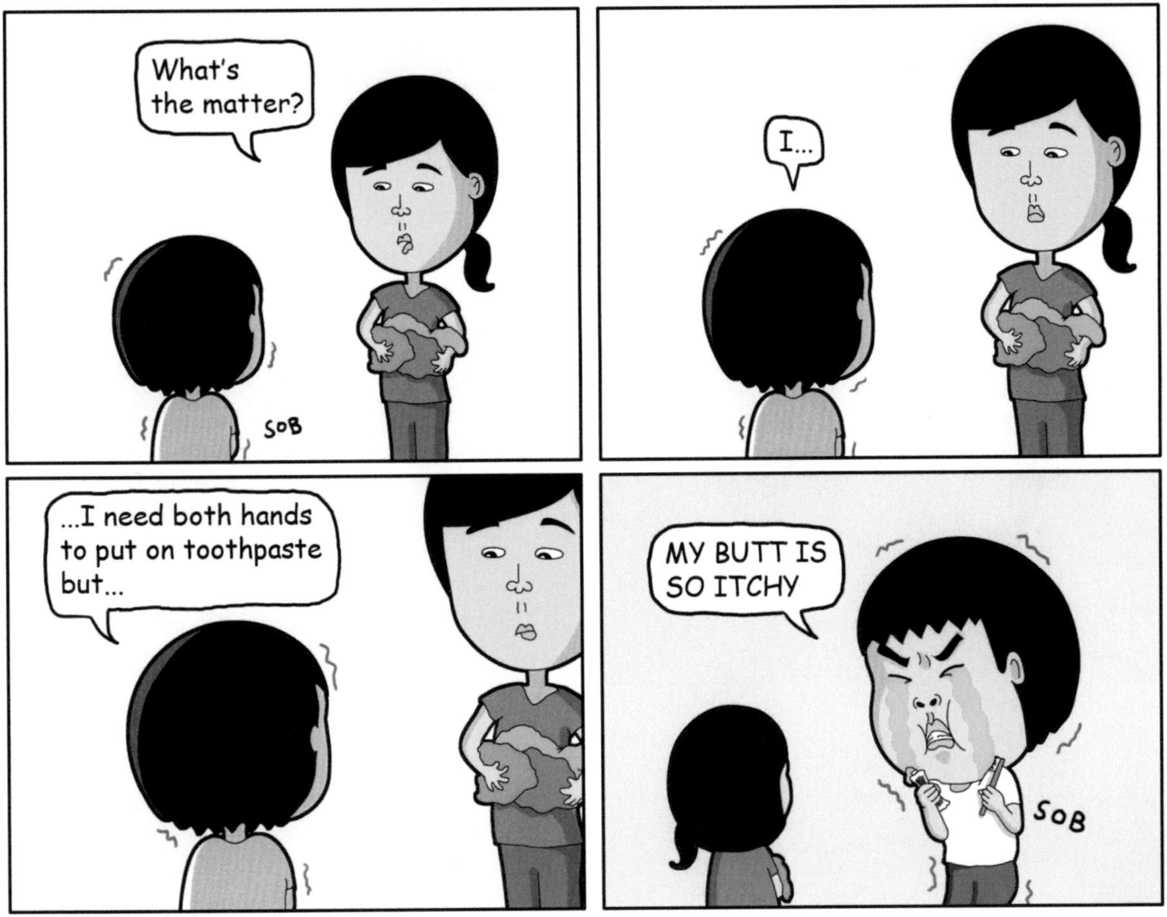
What's the matter?
SOB
I...
...I need both hands to put on toothpaste but...
MY BUTT IS SO ITCHY
SOB

Samuel, don't you think you look just like daddy?
I don't know I can't see my face.

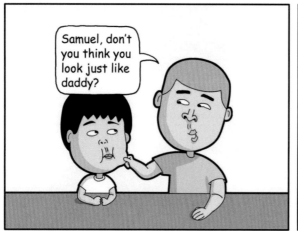

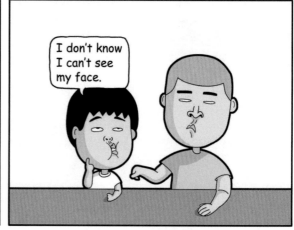

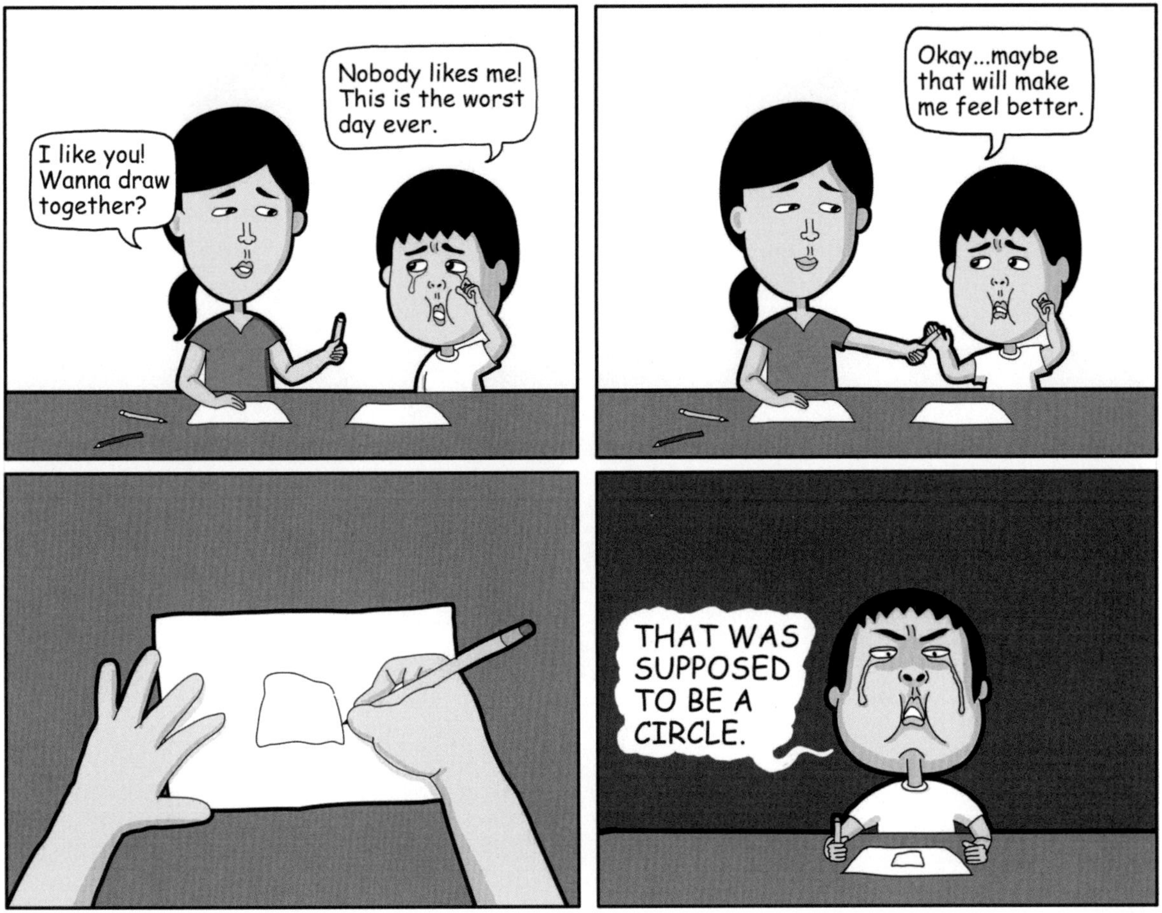
I like you! Wanna draw together?
Nobody likes me! This is the worst day ever.
Okay...maybe that will make me feel better.
THAT WAS SUPPOSED TO BE A CIRCLE.

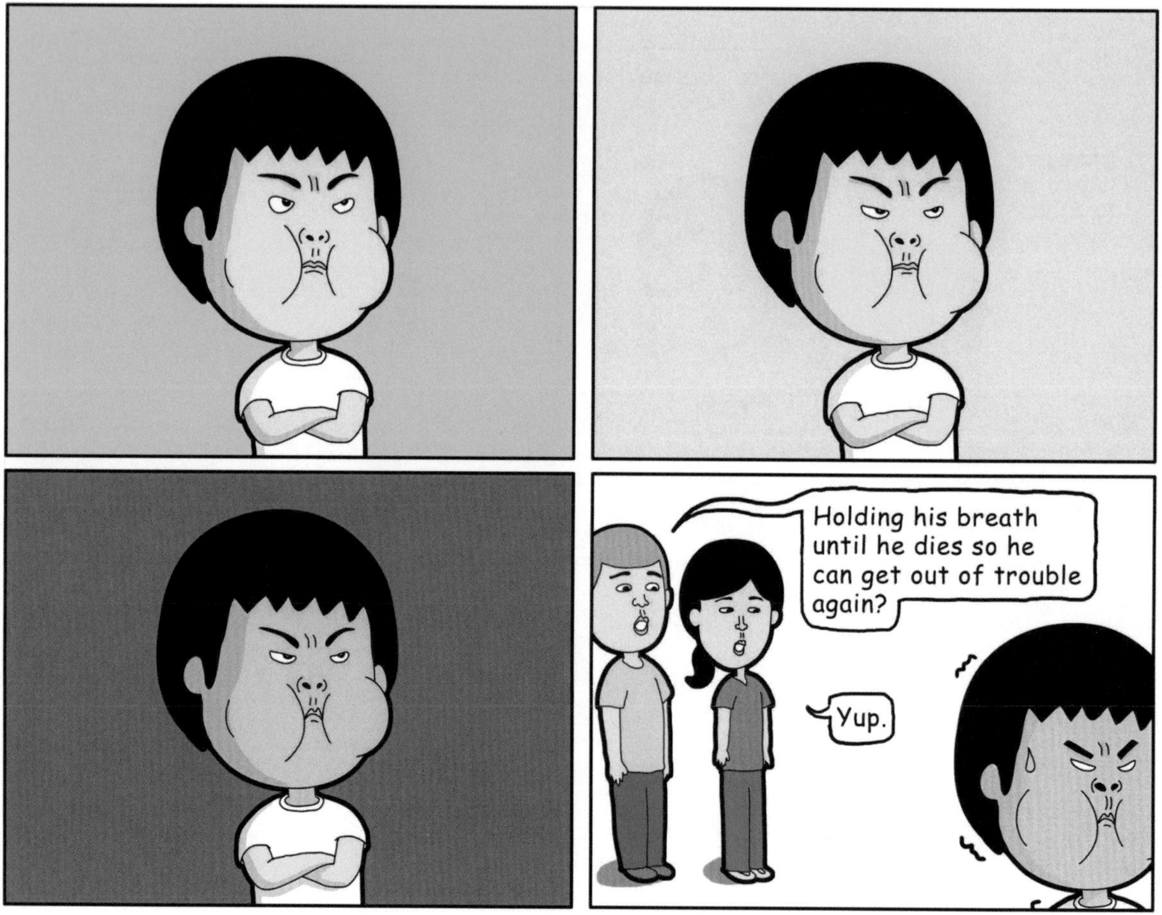
Holding his breath until he dies so he can get out of trouble again?
Yup.

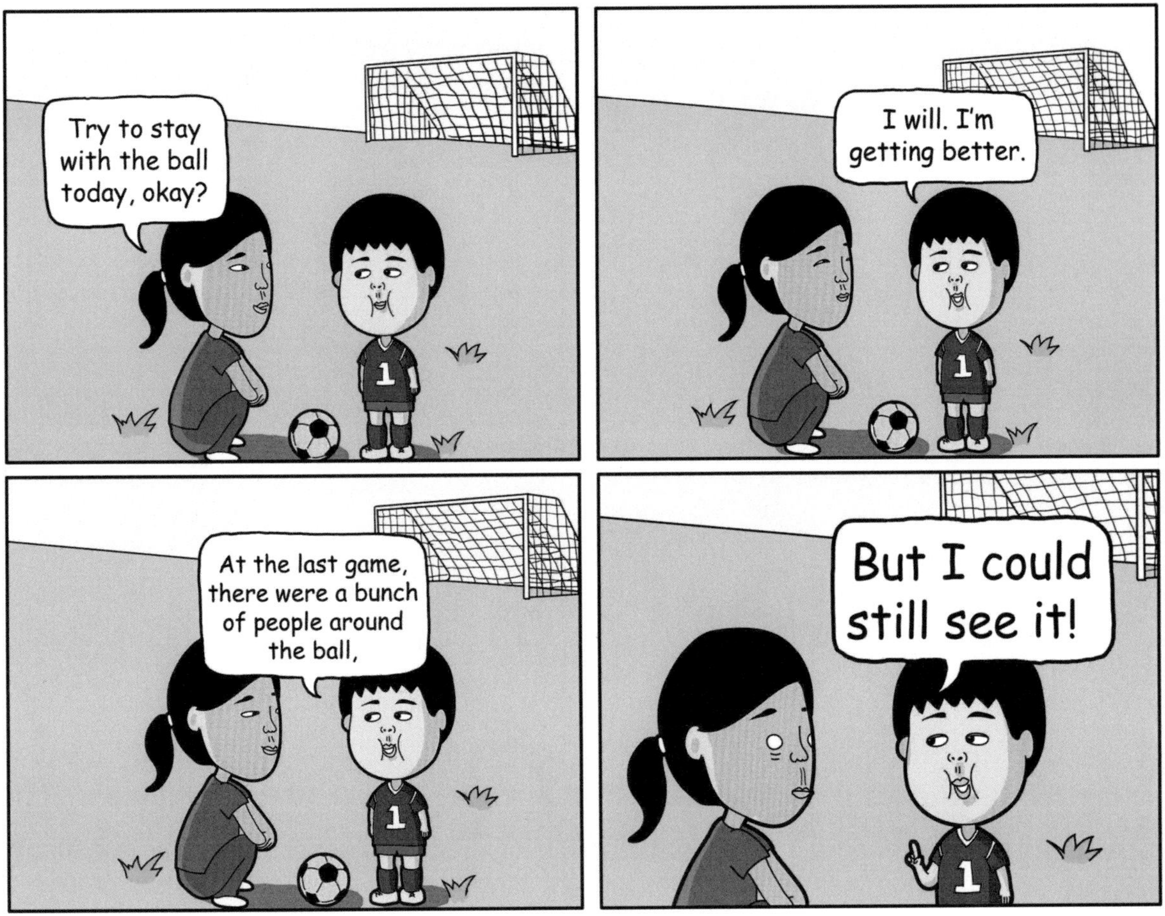
Try to stay with the ball today, okay?
I will. I'm getting better.
At the last game, there were a bunch of people around the ball,
But I could still see it!

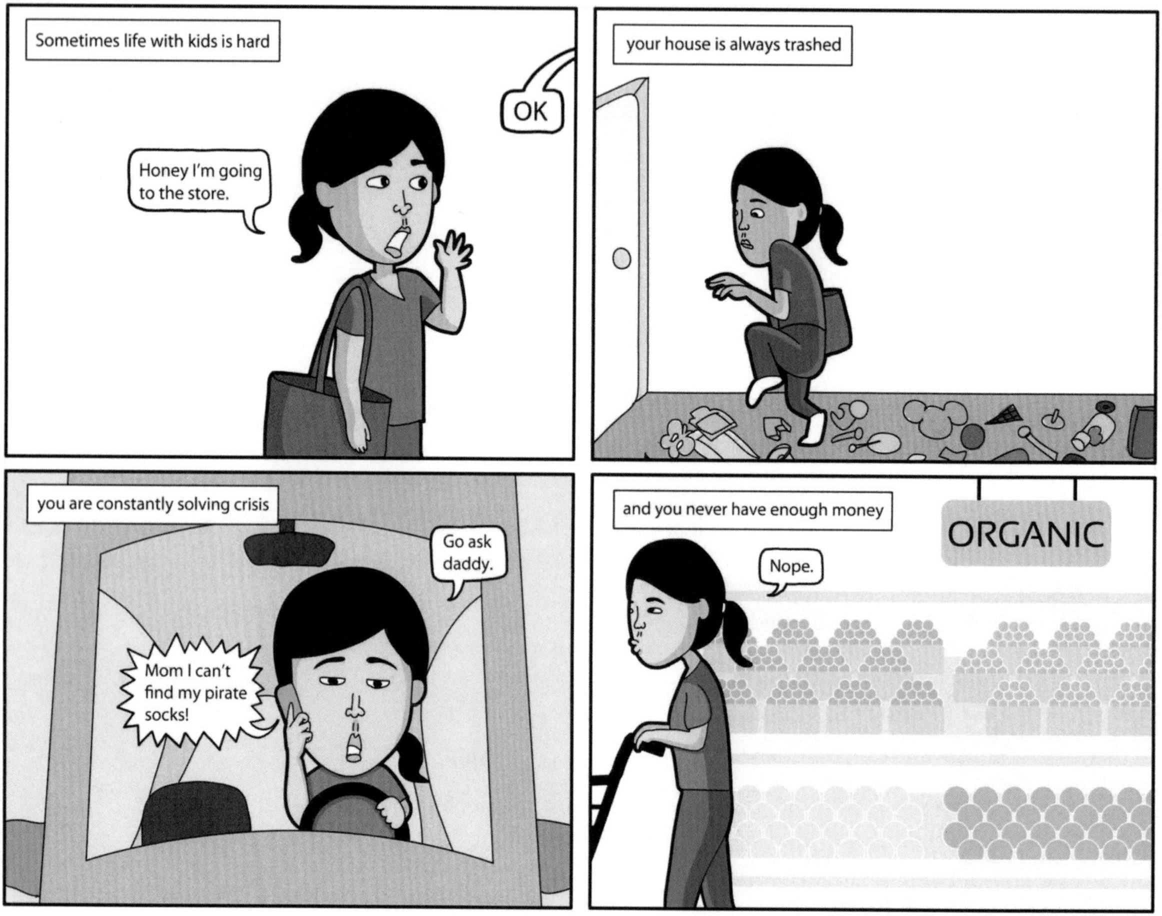
Sometimes life with kids is hard
Honey I'm going to the store.
OK
your house is always trashed
you are constantly solving crisis
Go ask daddy.
Mom I can't find my pirate socks!
and you never have enough money
ORGANIC
Nope.

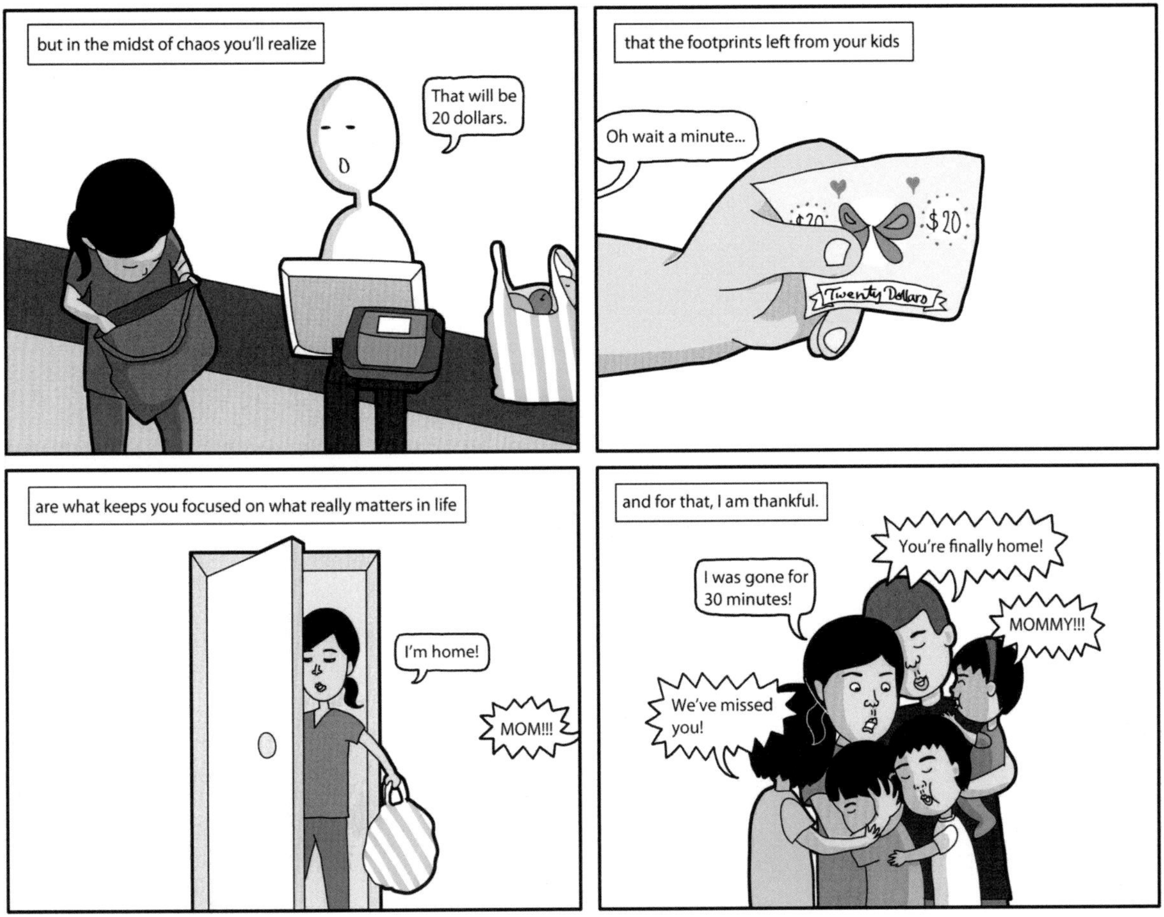
but in the midst of chaos you'll realize
That will be 20 dollars.
that the footprints left from your kids
Oh wait a minute...
$20
Twenty Dollars
are what keeps you focused on what really matters in life
I'm home!
MOM!!!
and for that, I am thankful.
You're finally home!
I was gone for 30 minutes!
MOMMY!!!
We've missed you!

Samuelism
C Starts With Cookie

ISBN: 978-1-5407-2974-3

Samuelism.com

Made in the USA
Middletown, DE
23 February 2017